Africa's Lost Leader:
South Africa's continental role since apartheid

James Hamill

Africa's Lost Leader:
South Africa's continental role since apartheid

James Hamill

⌠IISS The International Institute for Strategic Studies

The International Institute for Strategic Studies

Arundel House | 6 Temple Place | London | WC2R 2PG | UK

First published January 2018 **Routledge**
4 Park Square, Milton Park, Abingdon, Oxon, OX14 4RN

for **The International Institute for Strategic Studies**
Arundel House, 6 Temple Place, London, WC2R 2PG, UK
www.iiss.org

Simultaneously published in the USA and Canada by **Routledge**
711 Third Avenue, New York, NY 10017

Routledge is an imprint of Taylor & Francis, an Informa Business

© 2018 The International Institute for Strategic Studies

The International Institute for Strategic Studies is an independent centre for research, information and debate on the problems of conflict, however caused, that have, or potentially have, an important military content. The Council and Staff of the Institute are international and its membership is drawn from almost 100 countries. The Institute is independent and it alone decides what activities to conduct. It owes no allegiance to any government, any group of governments or any political or other organisation. The IISS stresses rigorous research with a forward-looking policy orientation and places particular emphasis on bringing new perspectives to the strategic debate.

The Institute's publications are designed to meet the needs of a wider audience than its own membership and are available on subscription, by mail order and in good bookshops. Further details at www.iiss.org.

British Library Cataloguing in Publication Data
A catalogue record for this book is available from the British Library

Library of Congress Cataloging in Publication Data

ADELPHI series
ISSN 1944-5571

ADELPHI 463
ISBN 978-1-138-54965-4

Contents

Introduction **South Africa as a hegemonic power**   9
Attempts at hegemony   10
South Africa's weakening position   12

Chapter One **Tentative hegemony from Mandela to Zuma**   17
Leadership, ethics and African resistance under Mandela   20
Pan-Africanism under Mbeki   24
Policy continuity under Zuma   33
Post-hegemony?   41

Chapter Two **South Africa's image problem in Africa**   47
Xenophobia in South Africa and its impact in Africa   52
South African economic expansion in Africa   55
South Africa's corporate footprint   60
Barriers to democracy promotion   65
Africa and the South African model of conflict resolution   69
South Africa's contribution   75

Chapter Three **The African Renaissance versus the South African Renaissance?**   79
Failure to transform   81
Implications of the failure to transform for Africa policy   86
Rise of Nigeria   93
A diminished South African role?   96
What can South Africa do?   101

Chapter Four **The plight of the South African National Defence Force**   107
Conflict in Africa   110
An ailing giant   112
Response to the 2014 defence review   119
Barriers to increasing the defence budget   121

Conclusion **South Africa in Africa: The challenges of the new multipolarity**   127
Decline and its consequences   132
A concert of African powers?   133

Notes   143

Index   167

ACKNOWLEDGEMENTS

There are a number of people without whose advice, input and support this book would not have been possible. At the University of Leicester I should like to mention the old guard or stalwarts of the department: Professor Jack Spence who introduced so many of us to the study of South Africa back in the late 1970s and who kindly passed on a wealth of material to me on his departure; Professor Geoff Berridge, the doyen of diplomacy, for help both professional and personal; Dr Bob Borthwick for his endless patience, good humour and company both at the university and on walks; Professor John Hoffman for his support in a multitude of ways particularly after the sudden death of my partner Lisa Bloxham in 2005. I also owe a debt of gratitude to the late Mr John Day for his kindness, support and inspirational teaching. Of my current Leicester colleagues, I salute the support and help offered by Laura Brace, Stephen Hopkins, Andrew Futter, Jon Moran, Mark Phythian, Kelly Staples, Helen Dexter, Rachel Tate and my former doctoral student Lesley Masters. Former administrative staff Renie Lewis, and Jane Russell also assisted me in a whole variety of ways throughout their time in the department. I also salute my former colleague Dr Jim Broderick for his entertaining contributions over many years. I would also like to record my gratitude to the late Landeg White, the former head of the Centre for Southern African Studies at the University of York, for his academic wisdom and kindness both during and after my time in York.

Beyond the university thanks should go to friends Charlie Bonner, Noel Melvin, Tony Doherty, Brendan Walsh, Bob Cheatham, Moore O'Neill, Jo Orton, Maureen Evans, and the late Bill Kelly for decades of fascinating stories, witticisms and penetrating observations on life and politics.

At IISS I am deeply indebted to the editorial care, attention and patience provided by Dr Nick Redman, Gaynor Roberts, Chris Raggett and Tom Adamson-Green.

On the family front, this book would certainly have not been possible without the support of the following: Lisa Bloxham and my two sons, Sean the philosopher, whose research work for me on Chapter 3 significantly lightened the load, and Finn who maintained a cheery and very wise detachment from it all throughout. Karen Logan, my partner, deserves special thanks for her amazing support throughout the project and for putting up with mountains of paper and with being an academic widow with huge patience and great humour (I will return to swimming lessons now!); the Pollak family – Marie, Robert, Bertie, JJ, and Grainne – for their invaluable research facilities; the Hamills – Sandy, Monica, Rory, Cormac, Tiarnan and Sorcha. Last but certainly not least, thanks and love to my mum Margaret Veronica Hamill to whom this book is dedicated.

South Africa as a hegemonic power

Despite the turbulence of its domestic politics throughout the presidency of Jacob Zuma, South Africa is still widely perceived as Africa's natural leader, principal conflict manager and chief international interlocutor on security and economic development. Yet there is reason to doubt the country's capacity to provide effective leadership in these areas. Although the intellectual case for South African regional leadership is compelling, aspirations towards this role are not necessarily well received domestically or on the wider continent. In the complex policymaking environment created by this resistance, the South African government's lack of strategic vision for a regional role has led it to engage in dangerous improvisation and ad hoc decision-making.

This *Adelphi* book draws on a rich post-1994 foreign-policy literature to explore the difficulties that South Africa has faced in translating its military prowess, economic weight and reserves of soft power – the familiar trappings of hegemonic power – into tangible gains and enduring influence on the ground in Africa.[1] The book argues that Pretoria's leadership position in Africa is being gradually eroded by a range of forces, likely giving rise to a new environment in which South Africa is not the pre-eminent power but one of several African states seeking to regulate continental affairs. It is unclear if this multi-polarity will facilitate the development of partnerships and a stable consensus for the advancement of the African agenda or else produce discord, fragmentation and gridlock. Regardless of whether it results in a concert of powers or a kind of non-polarity,[2] this process is likely to determine Africa's prospects for decades to come.

Attempts at hegemony

As Adam Habib has noted, hegemony – or, at least, constructive and consensual hegemony – can be established without recourse to domination, unilateralism or military adventurism.[3] Indeed, these practices form part of a crude caricature of hegemony in which a state behaves like a behemoth that is unconcerned with its image so long as it is respected and feared. However, no hegemonic project is likely to endure in such circumstances. Apartheid-era South Africa's unhappy relationships with neighbouring states during the 1948–89 period are highly instructive in this regard. Even in the relatively benign 1966–76 phase, which gave rise to then-prime minister B.J. Vorster's 'outward policy' and detente initiatives,[4] apartheid-era South Africa's attempts to assert a dominant leadership role in Southern Africa centred on economic power as an instrument of coercion. The government invariably coupled inducements and incentives to cooperate with veiled threats to neighbouring states. The implicit – and, occasionally, explicit – message to the sub-region was that non-compliance with South Africa's agenda would come at an increasingly high cost.

This relatively moderate approach finally collapsed in 1980, when the states of the sub-region rejected then-prime minister

P.W. Botha's attempt to create the Constellation of Southern African States – in which South Africa's neighbouring states would be locked into a dependent relationship with Pretoria and act as what were essentially satellite economies.[5] South Africa then began to shift towards a more brutish policy known as 'destabilisation'. During the 1980–88 period, an increasingly militarised South African state[6] ruthlessly deployed its considerable coercive resources – which included cross-border military operations, economic sabotage (both overt and covert) and support for proxy militant groups – to end Pretoria's isolation, bring the sub-region to heel and ensure that its neighbours could not challenge white power in South Africa. The project ultimately failed to achieve its core domestic objectives and may have even intensified South Africa's internal crisis, but in the process it caused enormous loss of human life and severe damage to the regional economy.[7]

The failure prompted a radical shift in direction under then-president F.W. de Klerk from 1989 onwards as part of his so-called 'New Diplomacy'. The new, democratic South Africa repudiated the philosophy and practices of the dark era of militarism, but still had to live with the period's regional legacy of suspicion, resentment and fear of South African power. As a consequence, much of South Africa's foreign-policy decision-making in, and engagement with, Africa since 1994 should be viewed in the context of the physical and psychological damage wrought by the policy of destabilisation.

Although apartheid-era South Africa was brutal and unprincipled in its application of power in the region, the country's efforts to dominate its neighbours should not be confused with hegemony. Unrivalled military and economic power may be necessary conditions for any state aspiring to a hegemonic role but they are not sufficient in themselves.[8] A hegemon, in the broadest sense of the term, aims to lead in a manner that employs a wide variety of foreign-policy instruments, and that inspires more often than it compels. These instruments include not only the capacity to deploy economic and military power but also values and ideals that have considerable appeal for other states. A hegemon will seek to entrench a set of norms and values while articulating a vision for the region that draws other states into its orbit willingly. It will also underwrite its leadership financially, and will be prepared to face down and discipline states that openly defy those norms and values – demonstrating a judicious blend of 'might' and 'right'.[9]

Although a hegemon inevitably prioritises its own interests, persuasion and coalition-building are also integral to the realisation of its vision. This will entail some compromise on its part – and, on occasion, even a willingness to surrender short-term advantage and play a disproportionately large role in regional burden-sharing.[10] The astute hegemon will always seek to project its own values as broader shared values, thereby establishing what Robert Keohane calls 'legitimate domination'[11] and, by serving its own interests, maximising benefits for others. Given the inherently unbalanced nature of a hegemon's relations with its neighbours, this process can involve a degree of unilateralism. If hegemony rested purely on cooperation and agreement, it would rapidly cease to be hegemony. Therefore, a hegemonic power will be prepared to risk unpopularity by departing from the consensus, if doing so serves both its own interests and its understanding of the greater interests of the region.

South Africa's weakening position

Judged by these criteria, South Africa has never been more than a fragile hegemon. Moreover, the country's position is steadily weakening: hegemony is becoming an ever more elusive goal as it struggles to maintain a leading role on the continent.

In the post-1994 era, South Africa could only have become a bona fide hegemon by meeting several requirements. The country would have had to view itself as a hegemon and be prepared to assert a strong claim to African leadership; acquire sufficient material power to make its hegemonic aspirations credible, as well as the ability to translate that power into concrete policy outcomes; and convince other African states to accept its leadership as beneficial for the entire region. The country would also have to demonstrate strong ideational appeal within the region, allowing it to build coalitions that promote core norms and values; and help stabilise the continent through the provision of public goods, particularly economic development and mechanisms to maintain security and order.

South Africa has failed to meet all these requirements. The country is hegemonic within the Southern African Customs Union (SACU) it established with Botswana, Lesotho, Namibia and Swaziland (albeit while encountering difficulties in its agreements with the latter three). Yet South Africa is only a qualified hegemon within the larger Southern African Development Community (SADC), and merely an important power in the wider continent – where its economic, military and ideational influence is in decline. Although South Africa's combined capabilities are still far greater than those of most other African states,[12] this advantage has not allowed the country to behave as a hegemon in championing and building support around a set of values, facilitating economic development, projecting military power or commanding the allegiance of other states. South Africa has met some of the requirements of hegemony by providing public goods, but lacks the capacity to do so extensively and consistently in both the Southern Africa region and beyond.

Peter Kagwanja's 2009 assertion that South African regional power was 'hardly in doubt'[13] no longer rings true.

As detailed in this book, South African hegemony is being undermined by a range of factors. Firstly, South Africa is reluctant to assume a hegemonic role, for a range of historical and contemporary reasons. The country has failed to adopt the mindset of a hegemonic power, often displaying exaggerated deference to the views of other states in the region rather than reshaping these views according its norms and values. Secondly, South Africa has generated significant resentment, suspicion and even outright opposition from other African states. Even within Southern Africa, there is no automatic acceptance of Pretoria's positions or leadership. Thirdly, South Africa has been unable to popularise its ideals in Africa or build a consensus around them. There is little evidence that these ideals are attractive to other African states or that Pretoria has done much to evangelise for them. Much of Africa's ruling elite has shown no enthusiasm for democratic values, prompting South Africa to retreat from the promotion of these values under Zuma and his predecessor, Thabo Mbeki, in bilateral and multilateral settings. Fourthly, South Africa has suffered from structural flaws in its economy, along with glaring weaknesses in the South African National Defence Force (SANDF) created by chronic underfunding. As long as it remains preoccupied with more pressing domestic challenges, Pretoria is unlikely to address such weaknesses, which limit its capacity to deploy well-equipped forces across the continent.

These factors currently present insurmountable obstacles to the development of a South African hegemony in Africa. In exploring South Africa's weaknesses, Chapter One of this book reviews the country's regional policy under its three post-apartheid presidents; Chapter Two examines South Africa's numerous image problems on the continent; Chapter Three discusses the country's need to focus on domestic socio-economic change, at the expense of a deep, sustained engagement with other African states; and Chapter Four analyses the shortfalls of the SANDF. The book's conclusion considers what may lie beyond hegemony for South Africa and the wider continent, a future replete with both opportunities and dangers.

CHAPTER ONE

Tentative hegemony from Mandela to Zuma

For the South African government, the construction of a coherent, effective Africa policy has been a priority, and one of the most demanding challenges, in the democratic era. Due to the myriad complexities of this process, the government's performance has been chequered. South Africa's official position – as expressed by each new administration since 1994, and articulated in successive defence reviews and government state-ments – is that the country's national interest is 'intrinsically linked to Africa's stability, unity and prosperity'[1]; it 'cannot escape its African destiny'[2] and turmoil across the continent, particularly in Southern Africa, threatens its wellbeing.

Conflict and instability work to South Africa's disadvantage by severely disrupting trade and transportation, discouraging foreign investment and increasing the flow of refugees and economic migrants southwards. Viewing the security of all states on the continent as interconnected, South Africa believes that it cannot achieve stability and prosperity if the rest of Africa remains blighted by underdevelopment, poor governance and intra-state conflict.[3] As they engaged in what Brennan Kraxberger and Paul McClaughry describe as a 'far-reaching recasting'[4] of South Africa's role on the continent from 1994 onwards, successive governments have been unable to insulate the country from the rest of Africa's problems – even though geography has afforded Pretoria a certain level of protection from at least some conflicts in the region. As a consequence, South Africa has tried to assume responsibilities befitting its economic, diplomatic and military influence by working in concert with other African states on economic development, conflict management, good governance and institution-building. In this way, Pretoria has sought to counter a narrative in which Africa is viewed, in the infamous *Economist* phrase, as the 'hopeless continent[5]'.

Anchored in a philosophy of enlightened self-interest, this may be a perfectly rational approach but it provides only a general statement of principle and not a route map for implementing South Africa's ideals. Thus, the country is yet to establish a role in which it can advance its national interests, fulfil its officially acknowledged responsibilities to Africa, generate domestic support for its agenda and avoid alienating other nations. Under pressure to achieve these goals, South Africa has struggled to translate its power into tangible foreign-policy gains, and its record in Africa over the last two decades has been punctuated by high-profile failures. In the 1994–99 Mandela era, these failures came in Angola in 1994, Nigeria in 1995 and Zaire/ Democratic Republic of the Congo (DRC) in 1997–98.[6] (Pretoria's 1998 intervention to restore the civilian government in Lesotho following an attempted coup was widely regarded as something of a debacle at the time,[7] but may be viewed more sympathetically two decades on because it helped preserve an elected government and signalled that South Africa would strongly oppose any military putsch in the region.)

In the 1999–2008 Mbeki period, South Africa had both successes and failures in its neighbourhood, the Southern

African Development Community (SADC) zone. The South African military undertook a major humanitarian operation in Mozambique in February–March 2000, rescuing hundreds of thousands of people from flooding and thereby projecting a new image of South Africa as a benign and even selfless actor.[8] Although South Africa was unable to push either Zimbabwe or Swaziland towards meaningful democratic change in the Mbeki era, it was partially successful in mediating the 2000 Arusha Accords, which brought peace to Burundi through a power-sharing arrangement.[9] As part of this effort, Pretoria deployed a peace-support force comprising 1,500 troops to Burundi between 2001 and 2009. South Africa also brokered an outline peace deal in a war-ravaged DRC that culminated in the July 2002 Pretoria Agreement, leading to the deployment of 1,400 South African troops as an important part of the United Nations Organization Stabilization Mission in the DRC.[10] Moreover, Pretoria helped build the transitional institutions, and organise the historic 2006 elections, in the DRC that flowed from the 2002 agreement.[11] Further afield, President Thabo Mbeki's attempts at mediation in Côte d'Ivoire in 2004–05 made a contribution to conflict resolution in the country, but they were ultimately derailed by the perception of the opposition – as well as the UN and the African Union (AU) – that he was too partisan in favour of the president, Laurent Gbagbo, for such a complex task, and this forced him to step down.[12]

Under Jacob Zuma, Mbeki's successor, this uneven performance has continued. Pretoria has been relatively successful in contributing to security in the DRC, and in playing a stabilising role on the border of Ethiopia and Eritrea in response to the 1998–2000 war between the two states. But these achievements must be weighed against South Africa's less effective operations in the ongoing conflict in Darfur, the confusion and indecision of its policy during the conflicts in

Côte d'Ivoire in 2010–11 and Libya in 2011, and its outright failure in the Central African Republic in 2013 (see Chapter Four). At the time of writing, there was little prospect that Pretoria would successfully mediate in the conflict in South Sudan, Africa's newest state, despite the close relationship between the African National Congress (ANC) and South Sudan's ruling Sudan People's Liberation Movement.[13]

Leadership, ethics and African resistance under Mandela

When Nelson Mandela was sworn in as president on 10 May 1994, South Africa enjoyed unprecedented global standing, a valuable asset in the foreign-policy toolkit of any state. This popularity stemmed largely from the personality of Mandela himself – particularly his ability to transcend his life experience by rejecting bitterness and demagoguery in favour of reconciliation and nation-building – but also from the nature of South Africa's 1990–94 democratic transition. Due to its unlikely and historic constitutional compromise – forged by multi-party negotiators on the highly unpromising terrain created by the prolonged political and economic crisis of the mid- to late 1980s – South Africa emerged as a state that had no enemies and could draw upon a vast reservoir of international goodwill.

The country had moved not merely from 'pariah to participant', as Greg Mills put it,[14] but from pariah to moral exemplar. This transformation was so rapid and profound as to be virtually without parallel in international politics. There was also a powerful desire in the international community for a success story in Africa, given the continent's bleak post-independence landscape of economic decline, conflict, military coups and, more recently, failed states. However, as J.E. Spence has observed, no state's foreign policy is ever a *tabula rasa*.[15] Even the new South Africa had to grapple with the various ways in which the legacy of apartheid shaped and conditioned attitudes towards the country, especially among other African states. Thus, Pretoria's post-1994 Africa policy developed in the long shadow cast by the militarism and malign dominance of the apartheid regime. Seeking a definitive break with this history of destabilisation and cross-border aggression – in which South Africa became what Adekeye Adebajo calls a 'regional *tsotsi*' (outlaw)[16] – the Mandela government engendered a culture of caution and restraint by disavowing all hegemonic aspirations and expressing reluctance to project military force.

However, South Africa's considerable economic and military capacity combined with its new-found global standing to raise expectations about its leadership potential. Much of the international community, particularly Western states, saw South Africa as well equipped to play a dynamic role in Africa by promoting conflict resolution and economic development, and by acting as a standard-bearer for democracy and human rights. Yet the perception of South Africa as the continent's 'indispensable nation' was not shared by all African states, some of which remained suspicious of its power and capabilities. Many countries in the region also resented the presumptuousness of a newly reconstituted state – particularly one led by a movement that had received extensive African assistance throughout its liberation struggle – believing it had the right to lecture the continent's veteran leaders on their political behaviour.[17] Since 1994, South Africa's rehabilitation on the continent has been complex and fractious for successive governments in Pretoria. As a consequence, the country has adopted fluctuating positions both within and between administrations in attempting to lead the region without dominating it.

The word 'hegemony' has been banished from the vocabulary of all post-1994 administrations in favour of the more emollient language of partnership. Yet, without seeking to formalise South African hegemony, the Mandela government nonetheless retained a strong normative dimension in its approach to foreign policy. Although his administration emphasised the need to promote democracy and safeguard human rights on the continent, it did so imperfectly and inconsistently. Indeed, Mandela's foreign-policy interventions were unpredictable to the point of eccentricity, often short-circuiting the bureaucratic chain of command through seemingly random announcements at press conferences, in interviews or in telephone calls with foreign leaders.[18] Other African states interpreted this behaviour as that of a state seeking to dominate the region and impose its values on others. In 1993 Mandela had lauded human rights as the 'light that guides our foreign policy'[19] and 'the core of international relations',[20] expressing the view that democratisation was essential to strengthening peace and security on the continent. He also brusquely dismissed the idea that democracy was somehow un-African or could not take root in Africa, arguing:

> Only true democracy can guarantee rights ... South Africa will therefore be at the forefront of global efforts to promote and foster democratic systems of government. This is especially important in Africa, and our concerns will be fixed upon securing a spirit of tolerance and the ethos of governance throughout the continent. There cannot be one system for Africa and another for the rest of the world. If there is a single lesson to be drawn from Africa's post-colonial history, it is that accountable government is good government.[21]

In pursuit of these ideals – which Graham Evans described as 'the touchstone by which day-to-day foreign-policy decisions were made and implemented'[22] – Mandela occasionally displayed some unilateralist tendencies that met with significant opposition in Africa. For example, in 1994 he unsuccessfully attempted to mediate between the Angolan regime, the Popular Movement for the Liberation of Angola (MPLA), and the rebel group opposing it, the National Union for the Total Independence of Angola (UNITA). He experienced a similar failure in 1997–98, when he tried to mediate between the Zaire/DRC leadership and its opponents – the Mobutu regime and the opposition led by Laurent Kabila, and, latterly, the Kabila regime and its Ugandan- and Rwandan-backed opponents.[23] Fatefully, in November 1995, Mandela proved unable to isolate and sanction Sani Abacha's military regime in Nigeria following its execution of Ken Saro-Wiwa and other Ogoni dissidents on the eve of a Commonwealth summit. The executions enraged Mandela, who viewed them as provocative, inflammatory and in breach of undertakings he had received from the Nigerian authorities.[24] The Ogoni dissidents had been found guilty of murder by a special military tribunal in a process that international human-rights groups viewed as deeply flawed. The episode provided an early warning of the kind of difficulties the new South Africa would confront as it sought to establish wider regional influence; it was also a stark reminder that an enviable global reputation would not necessarily translate into political authority on the continent. South Africa was rebuked by not only Nigeria but also the Organisation of African Unity (OAU), which said that its punitive approach 'was not an African way to deal with an African problem'.[25]

Although South African policy was driven by defensible moral instincts, the approach was tactically and strategically ill-conceived because it bypassed established OAU processes and structures. It also demonstrated a naivety about African diplomacy, prompting a backlash that isolated Pretoria from the rest of the continent and led one Nigerian minister to describe South Africa as 'a white state with a black leader'.[26] The following year, South Africa retreated from its hardline position on Nigeria by declaring the policy to be incompatible with 'the norms of African solidarity'.[27] The shift reflected the growing influence of Mbeki, then-deputy president, on South African foreign policy well before his appointment as president in June 1999.

Despite its occasional unilateralist impulses, the Mandela administration maintained a strong commitment to multilateral organisations and initiatives. In 1995 Pretoria played a key role in helping shore up and extend the Nuclear Non-Proliferation Treaty (NPT), working to bridge the differences between North and South over the future of the agreement. South Africa gave its firm support to the 1998 Rome Statute, which led to the creation of the International Criminal Court (ICC) in 2002, a landmark development in the prosecution of human-rights abusers, including heads of state. There is no persuasive evidence that South Africa made a meaningful pitch for hegemonic regional leadership in the Mandela era. (The intervention in Lesotho can be regarded as *sui generis* because the country is encircled by, and completely dependent on, South Africa; thus, the operation failed to serve as a template for a more assertive and interventionist policy elsewhere in Africa.)[28] Indeed, in the same year as the adoption of the Rome Statute, Pretoria stridently opposed the military intervention in the DRC, in support of the Kabila regime, by SADC members Angola, Zimbabwe and Namibia.[29]

Pan-Africanism under Mbeki

Although Mbeki never formally repudiated the Mandela administration's policy of 'universalism' – through which Pretoria sought relationships of equal merit with all states – he initiated a distinct shift in the emphasis and tone of South Africa's strategic priorities, particularly in relation to the rest of the continent. He adopted a more considered focus on all of Africa rather than just the SADC zone and began to robustly reassert the country's African identity as the central pillar of his foreign policy. He prioritised the attempt to rebuild South Africa's standing in Africa, which had been eroded during the Mandela era by the inaccurate but widespread perception that the country was, to quote Adebajo, a 'Western Trojan horse'.[30] This view of South Africa as a proxy to whom the United States had subcontracted responsibility for the management of the continent cannot withstand close scrutiny, particularly given the numerous policy disputes between the Mandela and Clinton administrations. These disagreements related to security issues such as South Africa's tepid response to the ill-fated US African Crisis Response Initiative; trade and aid policy; radical reductions in the US aid budget to Africa; and South Africa's determination to maintain close relations with Cuba, Libya and Iran, which Washington characterised as 'rogue states'.[31] Ironically, the claim that democratic South Africa had an ambiguous African identity strongly resembled an oft-used criticism of the apartheid state as being *in* but not truly *of* Africa.

In response to this claim, Mbeki – who concentrated decision-making power in the presidency to a much greater degree than his predecessor – shifted foreign policy in a more overtly multilateralist direction, developing partnerships with key African powers such as Nigeria, Ghana, Algeria, Mozambique and Tanzania.[32] The Mbeki administration greatly emphasised collective endeavours to build institutions and address African issues, a trajectory captured by the now familiar refrain of 'African solutions to African problems'. Multilateralism came to be viewed as both a principle and an instrument of South African foreign policy, as expressions of South African exceptionalism became more muted. Policy was firmly rooted within a pan-Africanist discourse, as well as an African realpolitik that recognised South Africa's limited influence and attempted to forge an African consensus on contentious issues, thereby avoiding any further debacles like that involving the Abacha regime in 1995.

In this way, the Mbeki administration exercised South African leadership discreetly and with circumspection, clearly signalling that its material power relative to the rest of the continent would not be used to promote narrow self-interest.[33] Thus, Pretoria proceeded in partnership with other major African states on issues such as the development in 2001 of the New Partnership for Africa's Development (NEPAD); the formation in 2002 of the AU as a replacement for the OAU (which had failed to move the continent forward); and the subsequent construction, under the auspices of the AU, of an African Peace and Security Architecture to facilitate conflict management on the continent. These institutions stemmed from a grand bargain with the West and provided, in Ian Taylor's phrase, a 'supposed blueprint for Africa's regeneration'[34] in which countries on the continent agreed to embrace economic reform, democratisation, the rule of law, good governance and anti-corruption measures – with the African Peer Review Mechanism (APRM) in place to encourage their compliance. In exchange, these countries would receive greater market access and a substantial infusion of Western investment and development assistance. The approach was designed to give institutional and policy substance to Mbeki's vision of an 'African Renaissance', a political, economic and cultural rejuvenation that would counteract ingrained pessimism about the continent's prospects. First articulated in 1997, this vision became the flagship of his foreign policy after he was appointed president.[35]

Mbeki's reorientation of South African policy initially appeared to succeed on two separate, perhaps contradictory,

fronts. It helped improve South Africa's hitherto question-
able African credentials among the continent's elites, but also
appeared to confirm the country's role as a regional norm
entrepreneur seeking to promote its democratic values as wider
African values – the behaviour of a classic hegemon. This apparent contradiction may explain the vocal opposition to NEPAD
from Libya's Colonel Muammar Gadhafi and Zimbabwe's
Robert Mugabe, who regarded the initiative as originating in an
uncritical embrace of Western economic and political prescrip-
tions. Similarly, the South African left viewed the formation
of NEPAD as an attempt to project the Mbeki government's
neoliberal economics onto the wider continent.[36] However,
this balancing act eventually proved untenable and, for Mbeki,
undesirable. His reorientation of South Africa occurred not
only at the expense of a foreign policy driven by ethics – an
unrealisable ambition in even the most benign global environment – but also of any meaningful commitment to human
rights and democracy, despite their initial importance as core
components of NEPAD and the African Renaissance.

Mbeki increasingly emphasised what Gerrit Olivier has
described as an 'operational pragmatism',[37] which prioritised
solidarity between African regimes as integral to a broader
pan-African solidarity through a foreign policy cast in an anti-
imperialist rather than human-rights mould. This shift could
be seen in South Africa's opposition to US hegemony – with
relations between Washington and Pretoria reaching a low
point following the 2003 US invasion of Iraq – and to structural global inequalities, with power and wealth still overly
concentrated in Western hands. The Mbeki administration also
campaigned for the reform of institutions of global governance:
the UN Security Council, the International Monetary Fund, the
World Bank and the World Trade Organisation (WTO). Reform
was designed to give greater weight to the voice of the Global

South, particularly Africa, and to help create, in Adam Habib's words, 'an enabling environment for African development' and a more 'just global order'.[38]

In 2002–08 Mbeki effectively steered South Africa away from the more nuanced North–South bridge-building role, and various diplomatic initiatives associated with middle-power activism, he had inherited from Mandela. Yet these initiatives had led to some high-profile foreign-policy achievements – among them a deal on the highly contentious issues surrounding the bombing of Pan Am Flight 103 over Lockerbie in December 1988, which killed 270 people. The deal provided for the trial of the Libyan suspects in the Netherlands, a neutral state, but under Scottish law and the jurisdiction of Scottish judges. This arrangement proved acceptable to both Gadhafi's Libya and its opponents in the dispute, the US and UK governments.[39] This period in which South Africa had an outsized global influence gave way to one shaped by Mbeki's more 'Southern' and ideological view of international relations. Pretoria's efforts to pursue an African Renaissance, not least its defence of the Zimbabwean African National Union–Patriotic Front (ZANU–PF) regime as Zimbabwe experienced violence and economic collapse from 2000 onwards, became platforms for an increasingly shrill anti-Western rhetoric. Mbeki articulated his firm opposition to what he called 'global apartheid' and the perpetuation of structural inequalities in the international system. Some observers viewed the approach as a contrived attempt to present South Africa as a reliable, even militant, leader of Africa and the broader Global South, and to erase the pro-Western reputation it had acquired under Mandela. Others perceived Mbeki's anti-imperialist discourse as a cynical exercise designed to obscure the neoliberal conformity of the country's Growth, Employment and Redistribution strategy – a 1996 macroeconomic policy of which Mbeki was the principal author – and to placate radical constituencies within and beyond the ruling ANC. Indeed, the academic Patrick Bond, among others, described the approach as 'talk left, walk right'.[40] Regardless of his motives, the president's rhetoric jarred with the more pragmatic position he had previously adopted, in which his campaign for the reform of the international system combined with a simultaneous and quite sophisticated attempt to engage constructively within that system.

To Mbeki's credit, his campaign for a more just global order helped push the debate on African development and indebtedness to the top of the global agenda at a series of G8 summits in Kananaskis, in Canada (2002); Evian-les-Bains, in France (2003); Sea Island, in the US (2004); and Gleneagles, in the United Kingdom (2005).[41] In effect, Mbeki sought the democratisation of inter-state relations at the expense of the democratisation of intra-state relations, as the former united African opinion while the latter would have been destabilising. He also mounted a defence of the Westphalian ideals of state sovereignty and non-interference, which, in the post-Cold War era, had been transformed from rights that were sacrosanct and absolute into those qualified by human-rights concerns.[42] This process peaked at the 2005 World Summit, at which the UN endorsed the position that the international community had a Responsibility to Protect (R2P) civilian populations threatened by genocide or other grave human-rights abuses perpetrated by their governments, or which their governments were power-less to prevent.[43] South Africa had fully supported this position, with Mbeki endorsing Mandela's view that sovereignty should not be used as a shield to legitimise slaughter and tyranny but should be embedded within notions of accountability and responsibility. In short, sovereignty should now be considered conditional. The AU, of which Mbeki was a founding father, embraced the essential principles of R2P – or 'non-indifference' as the organisation preferred to call it – even before the UN did so.[44] However, somewhat paradoxically, South Africa returned to a more restrictive and less enlightened definition of sovereignty following the World Summit. This signalled a retreat from an emancipatory model of pan-Africanism, as well as from the vision of an African Renaissance anchored in the rights of citizens rather than the rights of states and the often-oppressive elites controlling them.[45]

South Africa's more conservative approach can be seen in its voting record as a non-permanent member of the UN Security Council in 2007–08. The country protected from censure notorious human-rights abusers such as the governments of Myanmar, Belarus, Iran, North Korea, Uzbekistan and Zimbabwe on the grounds of state sovereignty and non-interference.[46] The stance risked jeopardising South Africa's moral authority and the international goodwill it had acquired during the Mandela era. Michael Gerson went so far as to dub South Africa a 'rogue democracy' for betraying the ideals that had sustained the ANC's liberation struggle.[47] As Olayiwola Abegunrin notes, 'there has been no greater or more successful derogation from that [non-interventionist] norm in the interests of fundamental human rights than the case of South Africa'.[48] Pretoria sought to justify its position by arguing that the UN Security Council should not have the power to address issues that more properly fell within the remit of the UN Human Rights Council (even though its behaviour in the latter forum was equally obstructive). But Mbeki also engaged in an instinctive defence of any African government facing accusations of human-rights violations, which he felt was an attempt by Western states to impose their own neo-imperialist political agenda on African states.[49] This tendency to view events through the lens of anti-imperialism rather than human rights was particularly evident in the South African response to the conflict in the Darfur region of Sudan: Mbeki insisted that the Sudanese government was the target of a sustained and hypocritical offensive by Western countries.[50] He supported Khartoum throughout his tenure, conspicuously failing to criticise the well documented human-rights abuses committed by the government of President Omar al-Bashir in Darfur[51] while condemning rebel activity there.[52] Mbeki also opposed the ICC's attempts to indict Bashir for war crimes in Darfur.[53] This passive approach to Khartoum's depredations could be at least partially explained by the deal reached during Mbeki's 2004 visit to Sudan – in which PetroSA, the national oil company, signed an agreement for exclusive oil-concession rights – and the contract between the Global Railway Engineering Consortium of South Africa and the Sudanese Railway Corporation.[54] Thus, a combination of ideology, economic realism and a misplaced notion of African solidarity eclipsed concern about human rights and Mbeki's African Renaissance ideals.

However, it was the South African response to the crisis in Zimbabwe that most neatly encapsulated his approach, with Mbeki including each of these three ingredients in developing his policy of 'quiet diplomacy'. The policy initially seemed to be a rational response to the ZANU–PF regime's descent into a naked authoritarianism when confronted by a challenge to its decades-long dominance from the opposition Movement for Democratic Change (MDC).[55] The challenge gradually led the regime to rig a series of elections, effectively abandon the rule of law and engage in unbridled violence against the opposition – a train of events that caused a national economic implosion.[56]

These abuses also placed Zimbabwe in violation of the SADC founding agreement, the 1992 Windhoek Treaty, which committed all signatories to the promotion of human rights, democracy and the rule of law while providing for sanctions against states who persistently failed to meet these obligations.[57] Pretoria's search for a diplomatic solution and attempt to steer Zimbabwe towards democratic and constitutional government was a defensible short-term approach, albeit one that risked allowing Mugabe to engage in further coercion. However, because Mbeki persisted with 'quiet diplomacy' long after it had exhausted its potential to facilitate democratic change, the approach steadily evolved into a policy of almost unconditional support for ZANU–PF. (He maintained the policy even after receiving unambiguous evidence of its failure in the infamous, and subsequently suppressed, 2002 Khampepe Report, which documented widespread electoral malpractice in Zimbabwe and bluntly stated that the country's elections 'cannot be considered to be free and fair'.)[58] This was accompanied by a visceral hostility to both the West and its calls for economic sanctions and the opposition MDC,[59] as Mbeki's position slipped into alignment with the African chauvinism of Mugabe.

The posture was informed by numerous factors: Mbeki's perceived need to demonstrate South Africa's independence from the West (which often entailed laboured efforts to play to the African gallery and flaunt his anti-imperialist credentials); the post-1994 determination to situate South African policy within an African consensus, which was treated as a virtuous end in itself; resistance to supposed 'neo-colonialist' designs on the continent, whether real or imaginary; a desire to uphold the sovereignty of African governments; and an instinctive solidarity with a fellow liberation party, however corrupt and repressive its behaviour in government.[60] Quiet diplomacy ultimately helped bring about the situation it had supposedly been designed to prevent: the entrenchment of authoritarian rule and economic decline in Zimbabwe, and the influx of as many as two million Zimbabweans into South Africa.[61] All of this stood in marked contrast to Mbeki's declarations on the fundamental importance of good governance and democracy in Africa.[62] Moreover, it damaged South Africa's diplomatic standing in the West as a reliable continental leader, exacerbating doubts about Mbeki that first arose due to his eccentric attempts to question the link between HIV and AIDS, as well as the value of anti-retroviral drugs.[63] South Africa's policy on Zimbabwe also provided an important break with the NEPAD contract, which rested upon an explicit commitment to democratic ideals.

Mbeki had come to appreciate the impossibility of riding two horses simultaneously. He could not position South Africa as an ideational hegemon, promoting his original African Renaissance vision, while maintaining solidarity with African states and adopting a bold 'anti-imperialist' stance in the wider Global South. He chose to prioritise the rights of African states and their ruling elites at the expense of African citizens, even if, as Laurie Nathan observes, the anti-imperialist project had been initiated in the name of those same citizens.[64] Mbeki's diplomatic strategy risked depleting the moral capital South Africa had accumulated in Western states, even if the emergence of China as an important African actor in the latter part of his term indirectly eased the pressure on Pretoria in this regard by providing an alternative to the Western model of political economy.

Policy continuity under Zuma

Contrary to some claims, Jacob Zuma has failed to make a significant impression on South African foreign policy since becoming president, and has been unable to articulate even the broadest contours of a 'Zuma Doctrine'.[65] This may be attributed to Zuma supposedly having a much greater focus on domestic politics than Mbeki, although his achievements in that area have been negligible. His presidency has limped along in permanent crisis-management mode, with Zuma engaged in a near-continuous struggle for political survival. Zuma also lacks his predecessor's uber-diplomat image and philosopher-king pretensions in foreign policy.[66] As a result, the Department of International Relations and Cooperation (DIRCO) has regained some of the influence it lost under Mbeki. More crucially, Zuma has always lacked the intellectual substance and body of ideas that might have served as a wellspring for policy development and innovation, whether at home or abroad. His largely squandered presidency has been shaped by the exigencies of the moment, damage limitation and efforts to muddle through. Zuma's policy inertia can be explained by the 783 allegations of corruption still hanging over him, his seemingly habitual capacity for scandal and his emphasis on balancing diverse interests within a highly factionalised ANC.

Given that his leadership of the ANC was secured in 2007 on the back of a so-called 'tsunami' of opposition to Mbeki's imperious style of governance and the centralisation of power within his office, a return to this approach was considered neither desirable nor feasible. Yet while Zuma could not be accurately labelled a 'foreign-policy president', there have been two key developments in his stewardship of international affairs.

Although his government stressed its continuing commitment to partnership and peaceful cooperation in Africa, in the early part of his presidency Zuma made a break with the more abrasive brand of pan-Africanism espoused by Mbeki during approximately 2002–08. Zuma's African agenda was generally less ambitious and he was less stridently anti-Western in his tone than Mbeki, suggesting that South Africa might revive its international bridge-building role. However, such a shift was complicated by the expectation among other members of the BRICS group – Brazil, Russia, India and China, which invited South Africa to join the organisation in 2010 –

that Pretoria would adhere to their collective position rather than attempt to meet Western powers halfway. In other words, BRICS membership likely entailed formal or informal obligations and restrictions that were generally incompatible with the freedom needed to act as a middle-power mediator. Although the Zuma government may have modestly rebranded Pretoria's Africa policy to focus on economic diplomacy rather than direct involvement in mediation and conflict resolution,[67] it has not significantly departed from Mbeki's broad regional agenda. As such, it is important to acknowledge the essential continuity in policy between the two administrations.[68] Zuma has reaffirmed his predecessor's commitment to the reform of global governance, conflict resolution, the promotion of economic development and a restructuring of Africa's role within a fairer, democratised international system.[69] In pursuit of these objectives, Zuma, like Mbeki, has been prepared to incur Western displeasure, causing South Africa to move into closer alignment with China, India and, perhaps less explicably, Vladimir Putin's Russia.[70] Therefore, it is inaccurate to claim, as some do, that Zuma initiated the current pivot away from the West in South African foreign policy.[71] As is confirmed by the rhetoric and positions adopted by Mbeki from 2002 onwards, the continuity between administrations is evident in several different African settings.

Firstly, Zuma recoiled from facing down ZANU–PF and providing support for a thoroughgoing process of democratisation in Zimbabwe. This was demonstrated by his strong opposition to Western economic sanctions on Zimbabwe – which included travel bans and asset freezes targeting key personnel in the Mugabe regime – and his uncritical endorsement of another flawed Zimbabwean election in 2013.[72] Pretoria maintained this approach even though Mugabe persistently manipulated the Mbeki-brokered 2008 national-unity agreement and often directed invective at both Zuma and his senior aides. Zuma remained in complete accord with the mainstream African position on Zimbabwe, seeming to confirm foreign minister Nkosazana Dlamini-Zuma's claim a decade earlier that, so long as the ANC remained in power, 'Mugabe will never be condemned'.[73] Following the military inspired ouster of Mugabe in November 2017, and the installation of Emmerson Mnangagwa as his replacement, South Africa quietly welcomed the transfer of power within ZANU–PF. This indicated that, despite the pledge of support Zuma made to 'the people of Zimbabwe'[74] during these tumultuous events, its principal interest remains the same as it has been throughout that country's extended crisis – the preservation of the ZANU–PF regime rather than democracy per se.[75]

Secondly, in February 2011, following the outbreak of a full-scale rebellion against the Gadhafi regime, South Africa voted at the UN Security Council in favour of international action to address the crisis. Although this may be viewed as a departure from the Mbeki line, Zuma would eventually return to the continuity approach. South African policy moved erratically from a clear expression of support for the action on Libya authorised by UN Security Council Resolution 1973 – which permitted 'all necessary measures' to protect civilians and civilian areas under threat of attack – to outright opposition once NATO began a bombing campaign to enforce the resolution. South Africa then moved in concert with Brazil, China, India and Russia (all of whom abstained from voting on the original resolution) to denounce what they called NATO-led 'regime change' in Libya.[76] The BRICS countries also advocated a role for the Gadhafi regime in any future political settlement, supporting the formation of a government of national unity in a manner that had become South Africa's reflexive response to virtually all African conflicts.[77] The Libya intervention prompted the return of Pretoria's muscular pan-Africanist rhetoric, with Zuma berating the West for seeking to impose its will on Africa. Meanwhile, in a blow to its aspirations to be the pivotal actor in such crises, the AU remained a largely hapless and peripheral bystander.[78] South Africa's approach can be criticised for its vacillation, immaturity and diplomatic naivety, particularly in failing to grasp the meaning of Resolution 1973. But South Africa did not remain outside the African consensus for long, quickly displaying what Simon Adams calls 'significant signs of buyer's remorse',[79] on the grounds that it had been misled by Western powers. Yet Pretoria's initial alignment with the US, the UK and France reinforced the African perception that South Africa too often acted as a proxy for the West. Ultimately, South African policy on the Libya crisis failed on every conceivable indicator, even if that country's subsequent civil conflict might be seen as having vindicated its position. Pretoria was unable to prevent Gadhafi from being driven from office and brutally murdered, while its reputation in the West incurred further damage, with *The Economist* describing South African foreign policy as being 'all over the place'.[80] The fluctuations of this policy also generated concern about its reliability within the BRICS, which it had only joined some months earlier.[81] Finally, Pretoria projected an image of incompetence rather than decisive leadership in Africa, even creating significant tension within the ANC itself where there was considerable support for Gadhafi.

Thirdly, the Zuma government displayed continuity in its foreign policy when it allowed Sudanese President Bashir to leave South Africa after he attended the 25th AU summit, held in Johannesburg in June 2015. This decision defied a court order that he be detained in compliance with South Africa's legal obligations as a signatory to the Rome Statute, given that the ICC in 2009 had indicted Bashir for war crimes in Darfur. Accordingly, the ICC ruled in July 2017 that South Africa had breached its international legal obligations in failing to detain Bashir.[82] The Zuma government also appeared to have violated South African law, which incorporates the ICC statute. South Africa's policy was rooted in an unwillingness to antagonise many other African states, which would have viewed Bashir's detention as a violation of pan-African solidarity and the rights of African leaders to travel unimpeded to the continent's diplomatic assemblies, as well as an attempt to support an ICC that has supposedly fixated on war criminals in Africa. In fact, the Bashir incident amplified some African states' determination to leave the ICC, a position that South Africa endorsed as it drifted away from its commitment to a rules-based international order in favour of the safeguarding of sovereignty and the prerogatives of African elites.[83]

On 20 October 2016, South Africa formally announced its intention to withdraw from the ICC, viewing membership of the organisation as incompatible with the provision in its 2001 Diplomatic Immunities and Privileges Act that grants immunity to sitting heads of state who are visiting South Africa.[84] The decision has become the subject of fierce controversy in the country – not least because it goes against its stated commitment to multilateralism and the promotion of human rights – but the fact that withdrawal is being considered at all speaks to the strong pan-Africanist current in the Zuma government's foreign policy. The South African High Court subsequently halted the withdrawal process, ruling in February 2017 that the government required parliamentary approval to proceed with the move.[85] However, this obstacle is unlikely to halt the withdrawal indefinitely, as the government has continued to insist on its commitment to leaving the ICC.[86] (When delivering its July 2017 ruling, the ICC did not refer South Africa's breach of its legal obligations to the UN Security Council, likely as part of a broader attempt to keep the country within the court's regime.)[87] 'In December 2017, the justice minister, Michael Masutha, confirmed the government's intention to bring a new bill before parliament to secure South African withdrawal from the ICC.[88] This was met with a chorus of indignation from local and international human-rights groups, who had hoped South Africa would use the opportunity provided by the High Court ruling to rethink its approach to the issue.[89] The Bashir episode confirmed that, despite the government's formal references to a 'diplomacy of *ubuntu*' rooted in humanitarianism[90] – and despite attempts by South African Foreign Minister Maite Nkoana-Mashabane to present South Africa as a country that 'will never shy away from defending democracy … in our continent'[91] – such considerations now have only a marginal effect on the formulation and implementation of foreign policy.[92] Moreover, the government and the ANC have persistently refused to recognise the inherent tension in attempts to reconcile pan-Africanism and South–South solidarity with a commitment to a foreign policy anchored in support for human rights, democracy and accountable government.[93] South African foreign policy continues to display a clear preference for the solidarity of African regimes, as seen in Pretoria's subdued response to African presidents who seek to scrap term limits and its abstention on the UN Human Rights Council's 2016 vote to establish an independent watchdog on lesbian, gay, bisexual and transgender rights. South Africa adopted the latter position in deference to the African bloc at the UN, despite the explicit provisions on freedom of sexual orientation in the South African constitution.[94]

BRICS entry
South Africa's accession to the BRICS group, formalised during Zuma's trip to the organisation's summit on Hainan Island in April 2011, has been his crowning foreign-policy achievement.[95]

Membership gave further expression to South Africa's commitment to a multipolar global order and, as BRICS members were
considered by some to be the next generation of global powers,
Pretoria viewed the organisation as having the potential to form a
bloc capable of balancing against Western hegemony. Accession
to the BRICS fits with a trend, first apparent in the Mbeki era,
of South Africa identifying itself as an emerging power that
adopted overtly anti-Western positions and sought to revise
the contemporary global order, rather than acting as a bridge-
building middle power broadly working within the confines
of this order.[96] Given the mixture of ideologies and systems
of government in the BRICS group – in contrast to the India–
Brazil–South Africa (IBSA) forum, which was established in 2003
and only included democracies – South African foreign policy
had moved further away from a normative agenda based on
the advancement of human rights and democracy, and towards
one focused on restructuring the global system. South Africa
was admitted to the BRICS due to its status as Africa's leading
power. Although its economy, population and geographical
size could not match those of its fellow members,[97] its presence
was designed to provide the group with an African dimension,
without which its claim to represent the interests of the Global
South would have been greatly weakened.

Yet Pretoria's approach centred on a paradox that DIRCO
recognised in its 2011 White Paper, *Building a Better World*.
South Africa's admission to a major international organisation
would encourage it to align with the rising powers of global
politics. Despite their pretensions and rhetoric on regional
unity, the members of the BRICS group may come to have more
in common with each other than with their neighbours, due to
growing disparities in strength and resources. The BRICS states
are not typical of the Global South: while they may see themselves as representatives of the developing world, it is unclear

how effective such representation can be.[98] They may profess to be 'agents of change'[99] in the international system, but their priority is to use economic and political leverage to secure a better position for themselves within the system rather than its democratisation per se.[100] Combined with the resentment South Africa's economic and military stature already generates in Africa, this pursuit of power will likely undermine the country's ability to act as the voice of African states in multilateral bodies. The assumption that South Africa could act as such a voice made possible its membership not only of BRICS but also of IBSA and the G20 (as the group's only African member), as well as its privileged access to 'green room' discussions at the WTO and its 2007–08 and 2011–12 terms as a non-permanent member of the UN Security Council. In short, South Africa's high global profile is intimately linked to the widespread assumption that it represents Africa and will therefore play a welcome, largely benign and uncontested leadership role on the continent. However, although South Africa endeavours to align its views with those of other African states in multilateral forums, in practice, this role has become increasingly problematic and controversial across the continent. Consequently, it is ironic that the post-1994 attempt to position Pretoria as Africa's natural leader has found its most enthusiastic backers outside rather than from within the continent.

Post-hegemony?

Since 1994, South Africa has displayed some characteristics typical of a hegemon, such as significant military, economic and diplomatic influence – although these characteristics have gradually waned. However, the country has rarely engaged in the traditionally hegemonic behaviour of setting the regional agenda, acting as a norm entrepreneur and building African institutions or regimes to entrench and formalise its power and values. The AU, NEPAD and subsidiary institutions such as the APRM (now a voluntary-participation system) are deficient in this respect, particularly given South Africa's emphasis on regime solidarity at the expense of upholding the democratic values articulated in the founding charters of these organisations. In the democratic era, Pretoria has always been strongly opposed to the deployment of its power to impose its values on the continent, but in the post-Mandela era it has also been reluctant to even cajole the continent into accepting these values, let alone to ostracise those who stand in open defiance of them.

There are three principal factors at work in explaining this more circumspect role. Firstly, South Africa has felt the need to compensate – and, in some cases, overcompensate – for its aggressive behaviour in the apartheid era by explicitly avoiding the use of economic and military power to pressure African states into acceptance of its grand ideological designs. Secondly, many African states – Nigeria among them – continue to harbour resentment and suspicion of South Africa, which is often expressed as a desire to assert themselves in opposition to Pretoria's agenda, lest they be further marginalised. Even within the SADC, where South Africa should be at its most influential, the country's power has been contested by Angola, Namibia and Zimbabwe – particularly demonstrated by their military intervention in the DRC in 1998, despite strong opposition from Pretoria. Even Swaziland, a tiny state governed by an absolute monarchy, refused to yield to modest South African pressure for democratisation and moves towards good governance in 2011, rejecting Pretoria's offer of conditional economic assistance.[101] Thirdly, while Pretoria has real diplomatic and economic clout, it has struggled to translate this power into desirable political outcomes. South African power is unevenly distributed across the continent,[102] generally diminishing with distance from the country, although, as noted above, geographical proximity has not always been a guarantee of success.

These three factors have reshaped South Africa into what might be best described as an apologetic hegemon. In fact, the country has been unwilling to either speak or act as a hegemon at the political level, even where, as in Swaziland and Zimbabwe, it has had the instruments of leverage and coercion to do so. Although South Africa has engaged in substantial activism on the continent, it is arguably inaccurate to claim that – as Jakkie Cilliers, Julia Schünemann and Jonathan Moyer put it – the country 'has been punching significantly above its weight in Africa and globally'.[103] Pretoria has certainly gained outsized influence beyond Africa, but not on the continent. There is also good reason to question Chris Alden and Albert Schoeman's contention that, under Zuma, South Africa has shed its 'defensive posturing' and 'made an unashamed claim to African leadership'.[104] Olusola Ogunnubi's argument that South Africa has displayed a 'subtle ambition to dominate African issues' is similarly problematic.[105]

Pretoria's diffidence in Africa has produced the very opposite of what observers might have expected given its relative military and economic strength. The experience of democratic South Africa in many respects subverts the traditional model of hegemonic behaviour. Rather than dominating the ideational realm and seeking to entrench its own values and norms – while using its authority, weight and appeal to build support for them – South Africa has instead sought to conform with existing norms and values. This reflects a South African retreat in the face of an open hostility to its ideals among African elites, many of whom recognise that democratic values strike at the very foundations of their regimes (see Chapter Two). Thus, Africa arguably suffers not from governments' lack of shared values, but from the often reactionary and authoritarian nature of these shared values, such as regime solidarity, non-interference and state sovereignty. In the face of this underlying political reality, South Africa has emerged as a tentative hegemon unwilling to impose its will on Southern Africa, let alone the wider continent. However, this effort to integrate with the African mainstream and exercise restraint has been an understandable, if problematic, policy. While making sparing use of the instruments of hegemony, South Africa retained the ability to draw upon them should the political currents shift. In other words, Pretoria had the capacity to engage in traditional hegemonic behaviour should it have chosen to rethink its approach to multilateralism and relations with other African states.

Nonetheless, within the space of a week in late March and early April 2014, two related developments cast doubt on South Africa's hegemonic potential, pointing towards a more complex and less predictable era. These developments – each of which highlighted an erosion of the material capabilities underpinning the country's claim to hegemony – raised questions about its capacity to sustain even the somewhat reluctant leadership it had provided to date. The first came on 25 March, when the publication of the *South African Defence Review 2014* revealed a marked decline in the operational capabilities of the South African National Defence Force.[106] The second came on 6 April, when Nigeria's economy officially overtook South Africa's as the largest on the continent, following a long-overdue rebasing exercise that put Nigerian GDP at US$515 billion in 2013. This figure, arrived at much earlier than commentators and academic analysts had anticipated, dwarfed South Africa's US$367bn for the same year.[107] Having suffered a serious blow to its prestige, Pretoria appeared to have lost two traditional lynchpins of the argument for its suitability to speak for Africa.

Although the Nigerian economy's new status is symbolically important and has generated considerable media attention, it is the structural weaknesses in the South African economy that present the more serious challenge to Pretoria's long-term strength and wellbeing as a pivotal actor on the continent. The steady decline of South Africa's military capability is also likely to pose a grave threat to what Schoeman calls 'its capability to set and influence agendas':[108] there is no guarantee that the country will remain able to deploy forces in peace operations across the continent, one of the defining features of its leadership. These developments should also be considered against the backdrop of two long-standing concerns about the viability of South African leadership in Africa, as well as its willingness and capacity to sustain the activism and normative influence associated with a hegemon. The first of these is the continuing resentment of, and resistance to, South African leadership across the continent; the second is the country's need to prioritise its domestic agenda above any obligations to the region (even if it cannot couch its foreign policy in these terms). These changes also suggest that a shift towards a multipolar Africa is under way, and that South Africa must begin to reconcile itself to the implications of this process. As with the passing of the 'unipolar moment' of global US hegemony, this new distribution of power is certain to create new opportunities and dilemmas for both South Africa and the wider continent.

CHAPTER TWO

South Africa's image problem in Africa

South Africa remains the leading state actor in Africa, but there is considerable dispute about what type of actor it is and should be. The country views itself as a responsible member of the international community, committed to working through African multilateral mechanisms and selflessly championing Africa's security and development interests in global forums.[1] This is achieved, so Pretoria believes, through the country's regional diplomacy; peace operations; high profile in the G20; and membership of the so-called 'outreach five' of the G8 (along with Brazil, China, India and Mexico) and of the Brazil, South Africa, India and China (BASIC) group at the COP-21 negotiations on climate change.[2] South Africa is also a member of the IBSA forum and the BRICS group, and is regularly appointed as a non-permanent member of the UN Security Council, as well as chair of the council's Ad Hoc Working Group on Conflict Prevention and Resolution in Africa.

In 2007 Nkosazana Dlamini-Zuma, then-minister of foreign affairs, said South Africa would use its 2007–08 term as a member of the UN Security Council to 'serve the people of Africa'[3] and promote an African agenda, particularly through conflict resolution and peacebuilding on the continent. In the same vein, Maite Nkoana-Mashabane, President Jacob Zuma's foreign minister, described South Africa's 2011–12 term as a member of the council as an opportunity to 'discharge its pan-African obligations'.[4] Zuma has identified cooperation between the European Union and South Africa – the only African state included among the EU's ten global strategic partners – as not merely an opportunity to promote South African interests but also to intercede on behalf of the African Union (AU) and the Southern African Development Community (SADC).[5] Pretoria frames all of its participation in global governance in similar terms. Indeed, Zuma views G20 membership as an 'opportunity to influence key policies relating to the global economy, and to represent African concerns and interests'.[6] South Africa's role at the World Trade Organisation (WTO) has been based on a commitment to addressing trade-distorting subsidies in the agricultural sectors of the Northern developed states and ensuring negotiations have a strong development dimension that moves beyond trade liberalisation.[7] South Africa also continues to challenge what it regards as Africa's underrepresentation on the IMF Executive Board for sub-Saharan Africa. Even Thabo Mbeki's strident pan-Africanism, and his repositioning of South African foreign policy within a multilateralist framework, were predicated on the belief that Pretoria was Africa's advocate and representative (although he always stopped short of claiming to be the continent's leader).

Western states have viewed democratic South Africa as a force for good on the continent, and the state best equipped to lead it, even if they have not always backed or understood Pretoria's positions. For the West, South Africa's democratic progress, relatively large economy, liberal 1996 constitution, voluntary renunciation of nuclear weapons and broader role in disarmament initiatives all confirmed its status as Africa's most important and progressive actor. However, many other African states resent Pretoria's paternalistic role, questioning its legitimacy to act as the leader and chief advocate of the continent. Their distrust of, and sometimes outright opposition to, South Africa continues to undermine the country's capacity to wield power.[8] Even the government's 2012 National Development Plan conceded that many neighbouring states see South Africa as 'a bully, a self-interested hegemon that acts in bad faith'.[9] This suspicion rests uneasily alongside an African expectation that South Africa will promote the continent's causes – a conflicted mindset that makes for a treacherous policymaking environment. If, as Chris Alden and Garth le Pere maintain, effective hegemony requires the weaker states in the system to accept the leadership and ideology of the dominant power – with that leadership and ideology being expressed through regional and sub-regional institutions – then South Africa has consistently fallen short of such an ideal.[10] In fact, the country's status as an emerging power, apparent anointment by the West as Africa's leader and exclusive membership of these various multilateral bodies generates at least as much hostility from African states as it does respect and support. Many African states suspect Pretoria of using Africa as a vehicle for its own global self-promotion rather than campaigning for the continent.

The BRICS forum has created a challenging policy environment for South Africa in this respect. Zuma argues that the BRICS group provides 'a strategic opportunity to advance the interests of Africa in global issues such as the reform of global governance, the work of the G20, international trade, development, energy and climate change'.[11] Fellow BRICS members see South Africa as their principal point of contact with Africa, and the state with whom they will work most closely to promote the continent's development agenda. Although this perspective led to South Africa being invited to join the BRICS group, the country's African peers view the organisation as providing a further opportunity for South Africa to pursue its national interests, to their detriment. They are only partially mollified by reassurances that South Africa is placing African issues squarely on the BRICS agenda – as it did by facilitating a broader discussion with African states through the BRICS Leaders–Africa Dialogue Forum at the organisation's fifth summit. Held in Durban in March 2013, the meeting was explicitly devoted to strengthening the BRICS–Africa relationship.[12] South Africa hopes to use the BRICS New Development Bank (NDB) – and its yet-to-be-established African Regional Centre in Johannesburg – as an alternative to the Western-dominated-international financial institutions and an instrument with which to direct the vast resources available to BRICS member states into Africa. Through the NDB, South Africa aims to engineer a structural economic transformation in Africa through the promotion of investment in infrastructure and industrial development. However, as of mid-2017, the NDB had only invested in the five BRICS member states, thereby reinforcing African concerns about the nature of the organisation and its motivations.[13]

Much of this resentment is part of the baggage that inevitably accompanies major-power status – power disparities often generate opposition, discord and even resistance rather than automatic acceptance and obedience. Indeed, democratic South Africa has struggled to counter the African perception of the country as a self-interested and opportunistic actor promoting its narrow economic and political ambitions under the guise of continental solidarity. Nigeria and many other African states have accused South Africa of being more inclined to talk than to listen, and of regarding anything that is in its own national interest as being automatically good for the continent.[14] South Africa's critics view it as a state that vocally challenges the global hegemonic project of the West, particularly the United States, and seeks to play its part in counter-hegemonic coalitions, while simultaneously seeking to establish a regional hegemonic project of its own. They also charge Pretoria with railing against global inequalities only to actively entrench the inequalities inherent in the African political economy. The feeling is that South Africa is seeking to replace the West as the dominant actor in Africa without modifying the unequal terms of trade, or disturbing the overall imbalance, in its own relationship with Africa.

Nigeria, Ethiopia, Uganda, Rwanda and Kenya all strongly objected to South Africa's uncharacteristically muscular diplomacy in pursuing the 2012 election of Nkosazana Dlamini-Zuma, formerly South African minister for home and foreign affairs, as chair of the AU Commission. Her appointment came at the expense of the incumbent, Gabon's Jean Ping. (Dlamini-Zuma remained in position at the AU until January 2017, but did not seek a second term due to her domestic leadership ambitions.) For many African states, Pretoria was determined to secure the post at any cost and showed scant regard for African opinion by ignoring established intergovernmental procedures for the allocation of positions. South Africa's actions departed from the convention that the most powerful African states should not seek the position of AU chair as they already enjoyed sufficient influence within the organisation. Pretoria rejected this unwritten rule in favour of the principle of regional rotation, arguing that Southern Africa had not held the AU/OAU chair since 1963. While South Africa contended that Dlamini-Zuma could strengthen and otherwise improve leadership of the organisation, some other African states suspected that she would push a South African agenda rather than an African one.[15] Pretoria's diplomacy around her appointment provided a rare example of post-1994 South African belligerence within Africa, a ruthless prioritisation of national and sub-regional interest above the broader pan-Africanist agenda.

Angered by this imperious behaviour, Nigeria and several other African countries intimated that they would not support any future South African bid for membership of a reformed and expanded UN Security Council.[16] (However, it was already clear that Abuja would reject UN Security Council reform that did not accord it diplomatic parity with Pretoria, a demand bolstered by the elevation of Nigeria's economic status in 2014.) Nigeria interpreted the outcome of the AU Commission election vote as a blow to its standing in Africa and as a clear challenge to its leadership that could not go unanswered.[17] However, the diplomatic fallout from this episode, particularly the deterioration in Nigeria–South Africa relations, would have been containable had Pretoria's attitude not reinforced a range of existing African concerns. Four aspects of these concerns are worthy of examination.

Xenophobia in South Africa and its impact in Africa

As noted in Chapter One, since 2014 Pretoria's approach to Africa has centred on a recognition of both the scale of the destruction apartheid-era South Africa inflicted upon its neighbours and the significant contribution these neighbours made to the country's liberation struggle. South Africa acknowledges the suffering this entailed, and feels that it has a moral obligation to assist Africa, particularly its immediate neighbours. As Alfredo Tjiurimo notes, democratic South Africa has sought to build good fraternal relations with African countries while positioning itself within the continent as 'an exporter of tolerant, humane values'[18] and a state dedicated to the advancement of Africa. Yet nothing has repudiated these noble sentiments – or undone the work of the South African government – more than the xenophobic violence against African foreign nationals in South Africa over the last decade. There are estimated to be between two and five million foreign nationals in the country, who have become convenient scapegoats for almost every conceivable socio-economic problem.[19] Given the economic and social deprivation experienced by the poorest South Africans, the influx of foreign nationals has triggered what Garth le Pere labels a 'Darwinian cycle of competition',[20] intensifying resentment over competition for housing, social services and jobs. This problem may have been exacerbated by some employers' use of large-scale migration to undercut pay and working conditions in South Africa.[21] The fact that some African immigrants run businesses in the poorest South African communities has only served to generate further indignation among marginalised people, although, as Steven Gordon's research highlights, there is no 'simple linear relationship' between poverty and anti-immigration sentiment, since many relatively affluent communities also exhibit xenophobic attitudes.[22]

This toxic mixture of deprivation and resentment has repeatedly resulted in xenophobic attacks in black communities. In May 2008, 62 people died and 30,000 were displaced as a result of such attacks, mainly around Johannesburg; in April 2015, similar attacks, principally in areas near Durban, resulted in six deaths and forced 5,000 foreign nationals to seek repatriation.[23] The impact upon South Africa's standing in Africa has been profound and far-reaching. The attacks have confirmed African suspicions that – rhetoric on solidarity and the African Renaissance notwithstanding – South Africa remains a state apart, and one with an underdeveloped African identity.[24] The country is perceived as having only the flimsiest attachment to pan-Africanist values and a minimal regard for African sensitivities beyond the confines of a narrow political elite and a black intelligentsia. The attacks and other abuses of African immigrants have been widely publicised in their home countries, dealing considerable damage to South Africa's reputation and leadership ambitions on the continent, as well as the country's broader sense of moral purpose.[25] African states have been swift to highlight the stark contrast between their support for the anti-apartheid struggle – and the sanctuary they provided to thousands of South African refugees – and the mayhem, destruction and murder visited upon their countrymen in a democratic South Africa.[26] For senior leaders of the African National Congress (ANC), the violence is particularly mortifying given that so many of them, as J.E. Spence notes, 'found succour and support in exile on the continent'[27] throughout the anti-apartheid struggle. As a result, South Africa risks a return to its status as Africa's pariah state. With the South African Human Rights Commission viewing the xenophobic behaviour as 'barbaric, violent and murderous',[28] even ministers in Pretoria anticipate a backlash against the country's political and economic interests on the continent. In some African states, campaigns have been launched to boycott South African goods, services and businesses, to press for the possible closure of those businesses, and, *in extremis*, for revenge attacks on South African nationals.[29] Considering that a central pillar of South Africa's economic diplomacy is the consolidation and extension of its role in Africa, the country appears to be committing an act of economic self-harm.[30] After all, the operations of many South African companies are stagnating domestically while expanding elsewhere on the continent. The backlash against xenophobic attacks jeopardises this expansion. The government appears to have been lethargic and reactive on the issue, doing far too little to address xenophobia by taking a strong and unambiguous lead from the top, or by addressing the socio-economic deficits that drive much of the violence.[31] Indeed, Zuma displayed a distinct lack of contrition in the aftermath of the April 2015 attacks, blaming the political and economic conditions in neighbouring African states for causing large-scale migration to South Africa.[32] Moreover, the government's post-apartheid immigration policies have tended to be framed in a 'foreigner as threat' discourse that has legitimised and emboldened grassroots prejudice.[33] The more cynical interpretation of these events is that leaders in Pretoria have knowingly deflected blame for their domestic policy failings onto impoverished fellow Africans.[34]

South African economic expansion in Africa

By 1994, South Africa was a formidable economic power in Africa, albeit a modest force globally. This created an enormous opportunity for the state to translate its material strength into economic and political achievements on the continent. Yet despite its relative economic weight, South Africa lacked a corporate presence in Africa and a dynamic trading relationship with the continent. There was some progress in this area during president F.W. de Klerk's 1989–94 policy of 'New Diplomacy', which sought to build a dialogue and a more positive engagement with neighbouring states. A cornerstone of the policy was an attempt to break out of apartheid-induced economic isolation by removing barriers to trade with Africa.[35] However, political considerations limited what a white-minority government – however reformist it might be – could achieve in Africa. Thus, when the ANC came to power, there was a widespread expectation that South Africa would develop its regional economic ties in new ways. The country's expanding economic role in Africa has been one of the most striking phenomena of the post-1994 era but, to the dismay of South African policymakers, this expansion has encountered a continental response that has been at best ambivalent and at worst deeply hostile. There is little evidence that South Africa's economic power has been translated into political gains – quite the opposite, in fact. This influence may have undermined South Africa's political ambitions, as Pretoria has been accused of pursuing self-interested, mercantilist policies that, despite its formal commitment to a more equitable regional political economy, have entrenched existing economic and development imbalances.[36]

These imbalances are most pronounced in Southern Africa: the South African economy is twice as large as that of the other SADC states combined, as well as four times larger, and considerably more diversified, than that of Angola, the next largest economy.[37] During 2003–12, South Africa accounted for 68% of GDP in the SADC zone, compared with Angola's 10%.[38] With grievances against South African policy deeply felt across the continent, attitudes towards Pretoria tend to be rather one-dimensional; recognition of its contribution to the revival of African economic activity is invariably buried beneath an avalanche of negativity. This economic expansion has principally taken the two forms identified above: rapid growth in South Africa's trading relationship with Africa, and the proliferation of South African companies across the continent. An exploration of both factors highlights the chasm in perceptions between South Africa's insistence on viewing its economic relationships in mutually beneficial terms and Africa's interpretation of them as neocolonial and predatory.

Post-apartheid South Africa had always intended to develop an assertive regional trade policy; by late 1994, just eight months into the democratic era, the value of its exports to the continent exceeded those of the European Union, at 22.4 billion rand (worth US$6.3bn at the time) compared to R19bn (US$5.4bn).[39] By early 1995, in a clear signal of intent, South Africa had 22 trade missions in place on the continent.[40] Although South African trade with Africa grew by 300% during 1994–2009,[41] it did so in a highly unbalanced manner that complicated the country's relationship with other African states. As Jakkie Cilliers notes, since 1994 Africa has become an increasingly important market for South African manufactured goods such as refined petroleum, motor vehicles, diamonds and electricity,[42] whereas its trade with the developed world is still largely dominated by minerals and commodities.[43] By 2016, the trade relationship with Africa was assuming ever greater importance in South African economic diplomacy. Three African states were now in South Africa's top ten export markets: Botswana, Namibia and Mozambique,[44] although, in the same year, Nigeria was the only African state to make it into the top ten in the list of countries from which South Africa imports goods.[45] Wider Africa is the only region with which South Africa has had a consistent and substantial trade surplus.[46] Indeed, Pretoria's 2012 National Development Plan called for improvements in inter-agency coordination to help create a more robust trade and investment policy in Africa.[47] However, many African states object to South Africa's huge trade surpluses, and the collateral damage they sustain from Pretoria's bilateral trade deals.

These are primarily Southern African concerns, as South Africa conducts the bulk of its African trade in the sub-region. The SADC zone takes 86% of South Africa's exports to Africa.[48] Within the SADC, South Africa's trade volumes have a ratio of approximately 6:1 in its favour,[49] with only Angola having experienced a positive trade balance since 2007.[50] Since 2008, trade in the SADC zone has disproportionately benefited South Africa. Although the country has accepted an asymmetrical arrangement in which its tariffs are reduced faster than those of other SADC states,[51] liberalisation threatens the future of embryonic regional sectors, which are unable to withstand competition from a more powerful, technically advanced neighbour. The Southern African Customs Unions (SACU) states – Botswana, Namibia, Lesotho and Swaziland – are highly dependent upon South African trade. Around 85–94% of their imports come from South Africa (63% of South Africa's total exports to the SADC zone goes to these states alone), while 68% of South African imports from the SADC region come from these states. Moreover, the currencies of Lesotho, Swaziland and Namibia are pegged to the South African rand. As a result, it is hard to dispute Fred Ahwireng-Obeng and Patrick McGowan's claim that while the SACU states may be considered 'juridically independent',[52] in reality they are 'practically economic provinces of South Africa'.[53]

To the rest of Africa, in which the trade imbalance falls only slightly to a ratio of almost 5:1 in South Africa's favour,[54] this situation appears to reinforce historical inequalities in a manner that is incompatible with South Africa's moralistic pronouncements on trade and the need for a regional policy which prioritises African development. For example, in 2013 South African exports to and imports from Kenya were valued at R7.7bn (US$798m) and just R240m (US$25m) respectively.[55] There have been clashes between South Africa's Department of International Relations and Cooperation (DIRCO) and Department of Trade and Industry (DTI) – two of the three government departments most closely engaged with wider Africa (the other is the defence department) – due to the impact of these trade imbalances on South Africa's wider political ambitions on the continent. While the DTI focuses on maximising South African economic advantage largely without reference to the interests and concerns of other states, DIRCO is more sensitive to their concerns and seeks to reinforce the message of mutual benefit and reciprocity.[56]

Some of South Africa's trade practices also highlight this discrepancy between the state's ideals and behaviour. Although Pretoria consistently speaks the language of South–

South solidarity, African states have just cause to question this commitment. By 2013, following the establishment of a free-trade area five years prior, 85% of intra-SADC trade was duty-free. Nonetheless, South Africa has continued to utilise a range of non-tariff barriers (NTBs) to restrict access to its market. These barriers may not have the same stigma within the current trading system as tariffs but, as shown by Phillip Nel and Ian Taylor, they have a more far-reaching impact. South African NTBs have the most significant effects on agriculture, food and textiles, which Nel and Taylor see as 'precisely the type of products that South Africa's neighbours would wish to export to South Africa'.[57] As well as impeding intra-regional trade, these barriers raise prices to the detriment of poorer states, reinforcing the economic dominance of the SADC's largest economy. South Africa maintained 14 NTBs in 2009–10, in comparison with the SADC average of four.[58] Indeed, all the NTBs South Africa imposed between January 2009 and June 2010 affected other SADC states and, as a consequence of such measures, South Africa was the target of more SADC complaints than any other state in the zone – 30 between 2009 and 2011.[59] Running directly counter to the notion of Pretoria as a champion of African development, these trends suggest that its rhetoric of solidarity is, as Nel and Taylor put it, 'merely a fig leaf for a destructive process that pulls the ladder away from everyone else, while select large economies progress, often at the expense of their neighbours and erstwhile Southern brothers and sisters'.[60]

Beyond NTBs, South Africa has tended to pursue a narrow agenda in trade negotiations without paying a great deal of attention to the interests of its neighbours. For example, South Africa entered into unilateral discussions with the EU on the 1999 Free Trade Deal having engaged in only minimal consultation with its SADC partners, despite the considerable risk that the agreement would damage its neighbours' interests. South Africa also broke with the unified African position at the WTO's Doha Round that any new trade negotiations should be blocked until all existing trade issues between developed and developing states had been resolved. Equally, Pretoria's enthusiasm for a tripartite Free Trade Area between the SADC, the Common Market for Eastern and Southern Africa and the East African Community is not shared by all Southern African states. Indeed, SACU members already have access to a free-trade area and struggle to see how this new arrangement would benefit them.[61] All of these factors create a strong impression that South Africa is prepared to plough its own furrow on trade issues irrespective of the opinions and interests of other African states.

South Africa's corporate footprint

The expanding role of South Africa's companies across the continent constitutes the second pillar of its post-1994 regional economic programme. Its corporate sector has taken full advantage of post-Cold War economic liberalisation in Africa, the vacuum created by Western underinvestment and the freedom to exploit business opportunities following the end of apartheid-era isolation.[62] While South African corporations struggle to compete in the economies of the developed world, their relative prowess in capital, technology, infrastructure and human resources, along with geographical proximity, gives them a competitive advantage in Africa[63] (even if they have had their share of failures in some African states, particularly Kenya).[64] As a consequence, the South African corporate sector is now active well beyond its traditional Southern African sphere of influence and is operating across a wide range of sectors on the continent, including retail (Shoprite alone now has around 170 outlets in Africa), manufacturing, transport, telecommunications, mining and energy.

As Christopher Gilmour has observed, this 'thrust into Africa is not just a nice-to-have, it is essential for future growth' given that the underperformance of the South African economy limits companies' potential for domestic expansion.[65] African governments have generally been hostile to this expansion, even though they have grudgingly recognised that South African companies provide an important economic stimulus in their countries, helping revive some economic sectors, build infrastructure and generate employment and investment.[66] Although Pretoria seeks to distance itself from the actions of these firms to some extent, their behaviour risks stigmatising South Africa and thereby undermining South African policy on the continent, such as peace and security initiatives or efforts to forge a consensus on political issues. In discussions of the South African corporate sector's northward expansion, the same phrases have tended to recur with monotonous regularity. South African companies are viewed as 'arrogant', 'predatory' and 'new colonisers' who are stifling local entrepreneurial activity and driving existing enterprises out of business.[67] Many South African companies have also been accused of exploiting high unemployment rates to impose cheap labour regimes, employing workers on precarious short-term contracts with no benefits or job security, discouraging trade unionism and failing to protect workers' health and safety.[68] These firms have also been charged with failing to embrace an empowerment agenda that would enhance the industrial capacity of host states by transferring skills and training local workers, and with maximising short-term profits rather than developing a sense of corporate social responsibility.

The fact that the South African corporate sector remains disproportionately white only compounds these problems. This reinforces the view that corporate expansion is simply an attempt to revive old South African aspirations of domination – establishing a constellation of African states with South

Africa as its hub – in a sanitised form. The resulting nationalist backlash against South African companies in countries such as Kenya, Tanzania and Angola has led to attempts to restrict their economic reach.[69] The backlash peaked in 2015, when Nigeria fined South African telecommunications giant MTN US$5.2bn, causing the firm to lose 10% of its value. The fine – the largest ever imposed on a company globally at the time and equivalent to two years' profits for MTN's Nigerian operation – came after MTN failed to meet a deadline to deactivate 5.2m active but unregistered SIM cards. The Nigerian authorities viewed the issue as vital to national security because the unregistered cards had been linked to insurgent group Boko Haram and criminal organisations. Observers have viewed the Nigerian authorities' punitive approach as a cynical means of revenue generation that could deter future investment in Nigeria, and as a way to hit out at South African companies who are widely resented in Nigeria. The fine also appeared to be designed to signal Abuja's displeasure with the overall trajectory of the Nigeria–South Africa relationship, which had become increasingly fractious under the leaderships of Zuma and then Nigerian president Goodluck Jonathan.[70]

Pretoria faces a dilemma on this issue, as the sometimes cavalier approach of South African corporations undermines its conciliatory language of partnership and balanced development. Although Pretoria does not bear direct responsibility for the behaviour of these firms, the distinction may be lost on African audiences for whom, as Tjemolane, Needling and Schoeman note, they 'mutually contribute to what is generally perceived as the South African 'profile' or 'presence' on the continent'.[71] As a result, South Africa's image may be contaminated by a mixture of festering economic grievances.

Most of the corporate expansion into Africa occurs outside any government framework. The state–business nexus in

South Africa cannot be compared with the close public–private coordination that characterises Brazilian or Chinese engagement with Africa.[72] In fact, the absence of any serious attempt to integrate the work of government and business with a view to creating a 'competition state'[73] is a source of concern for analysts such as Brendan Vickers, who laments the 'historical misalignment' between the two.[74] In 2009 Nkoana-Mashabane spoke of the need for greater coordination of economic diplomacy across government departments and diplomatic missions, which would require closer liaison with business to help facilitate market access.[75] In 2006 Sue van der Merwe, then-deputy minister of foreign affairs, called for 'unity of purpose' among government, business and civil society in projecting the country's image abroad – although her accompanying claim that business penetration into Africa had 'greatly enhanced our international standing' and was 'advancing our foreign policy objectives' may have been inaccurate.[76]

Nonetheless, corporate expansion into Africa is not driven purely by private capital: the state has actively supported the process through the Industrial Development Corporation – which has helped fund a variety of projects and underwrites risk throughout the continent[77] – the DTI and the Development Bank of Southern Africa. Ian Taylor sees this as the creation of 'economic and political frameworks amenable to accumulation', with political and corporate elites working in tandem to advance their interests.[78] Therefore, it is difficult for the state to fully dissociate itself from this corporate expansion and an aggressive pursuit of market access. Indeed, the South African state itself has an important presence in the African economy through the activities of its parastatals such as Eskom and Spoornet, each of which has viewed Africa's deficits in energy and transport infrastructure as providing openings for business expansion.[79] Such opportunism fuels resentment of South

Africa. Many African states see the projection of raw economic power by South African corporations – and, to a lesser extent, the South African state – as a crude form of hegemony. This perception jeopardises Pretoria's attempts to build a more consensual model of hegemony in which the country attracts support due to its values and its willingness to assume a dispro-portionately large share of regional burdens, particularly in the distribution of public goods.

Yet while this perception of South Africa as an overbearing actor is now entrenched in Africa, some within the country itself condemn the failure of politicians and businesses to prioritise the relationship with Africa, viewing the country's regional engagement as having been overly passive and cautious.[80] South African foreign direct investment (FDI) in Africa has increased at four times the rate of its global FDI – from R3.8bn (US$1.1bn) in 1994 to R115bn (US$13.6bn) in 2009[81] – and produces returns higher than those in South Africa itself.[82] Moreover, this invest-ment in Africa is relatively diversified, placing less emphasis on the extractive sector than that of China, Brazil and India. However, in 2015 only 20% of South African trade involved other African countries (an increase of seven percentage points from 2009).[83] As this left considerable scope for further expan-sion, some commentators have argued that South Africa's lethargy has allowed China, the US, Brazil and India to take the lead in FDI in Africa at its expense. For example, George Rautenbach bemoans the absence of a South African economic strategy or a 'well-defined vision for its relationship with the continent', highlighting Pretoria's failure to take advantage of state visits or to develop a deeper understanding of the conti-nent.[84] This reinforces Vickers' argument that Africa policy cannot be driven by purely altruistic considerations, and that South Africa has failed to secure direct commercial benefits, such as privileged market access for its companies, from its efforts at peacebuilding and post-conflict reconstruction on the continent. Thus, Vickers contends, Pretoria has needlessly ceded commercial advantage to other BRICS states in places such as the Democratic Republic of the Congo (DRC).[85] He also criticises 'Pretoria's failure to lobby effectively for industry'[86] and its general tendency to be overly defensive in the conduct of its African economic diplomacy. Thus, South Africa finds itself in an invidious position in which it is accused of being both too aggressive and too timid at the same time. There is actually considerable merit in each charge, with the private sector pursuing its African interests very robustly and often insensitively while the government, conscious of the diplomatic repercussions, proceeds much more cautiously. Unfortunately for the government, however, the South African 'brand' in Africa may be more associated with the former than the latter, not least because – for most African peoples – these companies provide their most direct contact with and experience of the giant to the south. This reaffirms the need for an economic policy towards Africa which balances the pursuit of expanding commercial engagement – a matter of national self-interest for Pretoria – with a recognition that this may be best achieved when combined with a commitment to social justice and workers' rights as well as a sensitivity to the interests of other African states.

Barriers to democracy promotion

South Africa's promotion of democracy and human rights has encountered significant practical, if not always public, opposition from much of the continent's political leadership. The values central to the South African constitutional settlement of the mid-1990s have limited traction among African governments; although South Africa's commitment to spreading these ideals has been ineffectual and limited in the

Mbeki and Zuma eras, they still generate significant resistance from African political elites. The South African model embraces all the standard features of a liberal democracy: the supremacy of the constitution; an independent judiciary; neutral state institutions; a free press; an active and autonomous civil society; free and fair elections; and term limits. These values require constant, vigilant protection in South Africa itself due to the tension between such liberal-democratic, pluralist values and the overwhelming dominance of the ruling party. Indeed, the increasingly chaotic nature of ANC rule since 2009 belies any complacent assumption that democracy will inevitably succeed at home.

In the Zuma era, South Africa appears to have more closely followed a typical post-independence African narrative instead of providing a viable alternative to it – a perception reinforced by a long series of exposés on corruption among the ANC elite.[87] State-owned enterprises – now crammed with ANC appointees through the policy of 'cadre deployment', which is designed to secure the party's control over what it calls the 'strategic centres of power' – have increasingly become vehicles for private accumulation. Due to endemic corruption, concerns about the capture of the state by private networks connected to President Zuma now dominate the political discourse.[88] In 2016–17, four separate reports – one from the outgoing Public Protector and three from civil-society groups – highlighted a ruthless programme of self-enrichment undertaken by a new parasitic class that has either emerged from within or become intimately tied to the ANC. This network is dedicated to plundering state resources and abusing state institutions for private gain. If left unchecked, this process will virtually guarantee South Africa's descent into an outright kleptocracy.[89] In this way, South Africa's global, regional and sub-regional reputation as a champion of democracy and good governance in Africa is being tarnished by the plethora of damaging revelations that have overtaken the Zuma presidency since its inauguration in 2009.[90]

The embrace of democratic values is also problematic in many African states, where their rigorous implementation would pose an existential threat to ruling elites. By controlling the state, these elites retain access to resources, pursue a strategy of predatory accumulation, establish patronage networks and purchase the support of clients. This misuse of public resources for private and political gain is the lifeblood of a neo-patrimonial system that is deeply rooted in Africa, drawing on informal networks of authority and running parallel to the formal political system. As such, elites are unlikely to end this misuse of resources in accordance with nebulous notions of democracy and good governance.[91] In 2004 Taylor described the difficulty of promoting democratic values through elites who have no material or political interest in them:

> The irony is that the type of good governance solutions advanced by NEPAD [New Partnership for Africa's Development] would deprive [authoritarian] rulers of the means to maintain their patronage networks. To have an Africa grounded on the governance principles of NEPAD would actually erode the base upon which the state is predicated. And yet we are expected to believe that the very same African elites who benefit from the neo-patrimonial system will now commit a form of class suicide. The possibility seems improbable ... the whole system is based on privatized patronage and the prohibition of real, functioning democracy – in other words, broad accountability. To begin implementing and operating by the rubric of 'good governance' would inevitably damage the incumbent elites' own personalized grip

on the system and reduce their ability to service their clients, inevitably leading to their loss of power.[92]

As a consequence, some African elites – and through them the continent's various multilateral organisations – have learned to master the vocabulary of democratisation, as well as some of its procedural rituals, while shunning its substance. In effect, they have become specialists in the construction of elaborate democratic façades behind which informal mechanisms of power and neo-patrimonial rule persist largely unhindered. Egregious refusal to accept electoral defeat may trigger intervention, certainly in West Africa (although it didn't in the SADC), but more mundane authoritarian and undemocratic behaviour is still largely tolerated. South Africa has adapted to this reality – and, under Zuma, increasingly mirrored it – yet the perception remains entrenched that Pretoria is somehow a 'democratic imperialist' presenting a fundamental challenge to an authoritarian African status quo.[93] In fact, Pretoria's commitment to democracy is now highly qualified: its default position is to embrace an existing consensus in which democracy is safely confined to the realms of aspiration rather than an indispensable benchmark of African progress. South Africa has shed most of the democratic evangelism of the Mandela era, whose principal surviving feature is its robust opposition to the unconstitutional seizure of power via a military coup[94] – but not necessarily the unconstitutional retention of power by existing authoritarian regimes. As is frequently highlighted by the ANC's domestic opponents, South Africa has settled for solidarity with a range of illiberal democracies and, worse still, states with no democratic traits at all.[95] In doing so, it has abandoned the role of norm entrepreneur associated with hegemonic powers, but without securing the full confidence and trust of other African states. Moreover, South Africa's retreat from democratic values has alienated the country from grassroots activists in African civil society while damaging its relationship with Western states.

Africa and the South African model of conflict resolution

It has become something of an established truth in the post-1994 era that, as Kristina Bentley and Roger Southall argue, 'the whole world looks to South Africa as the key model for resolving intractable conflicts after the experience of the transition from apartheid to democracy'.[96] This view of the country's experience as inspirational – South Africa as a 'universal metaphor', to quote Mark Gevisser[97] – is in danger of becoming an overly hubristic posture insufficiently attuned to the power dynamics at work in conflicts elsewhere on the continent. South Africa risks immersing itself in a bout of self-congratulation with a policy based on wishful thinking, ignorance and the complacent belief that its model of conflict resolution enjoys unconditional approval elsewhere. This is not to dismiss the many valuable lessons that can be gleaned from the country's rich negotiating experience. South Africans engineered a historic compromise in exceptionally difficult circumstances, with the rival elites demonstrating a maturity and wisdom that allowed them to move beyond triumphalism and a zero-sum game to fashion an inclusive settlement in which all parties felt they had a stake. Equally, there are many lessons to be drawn from a study of the mechanics of the South African negotiating process – perhaps more than from the outcome itself, in which majoritarianism ultimately eclipsed power-sharing or consociational approaches.[98] Given this undoubted success, it is unsurprising that South Africa sees its negotiated settlement as a template for conflict resolution elsewhere. But, as Kurt Shillinger observes, the danger is that South Africa will become 'blinded by enthusiasm for its own model',[99] causing it to misread the nature of conflict elsewhere in Africa and to overstate the viability of its approach.[100]

Contrary to popular mythology, the South African model does not enjoy universal adulation across the continent, where many conflicts are far from resolution and remain stubbornly unreceptive to Pretoria's solutions. In such conflicts, all sides seek the total defeat of their opponent rather than a durable accommodation, as their mutual enmity runs too deeply for them to contemplate negotiations and power-sharing. In these circumstances, South Africa's intervention or the promotion of a South African-style settlement are likely to be considered intrusive and unwelcome. Of course, the South African approach may become more relevant if the parties to a conflict recognise that they are locked into a mutually destructive stalemate. Such recognition is normally the prelude to serious negotiations. However, the parties may not recognise that such a stalemate exists and – even if they do – may regard it as temporary and harbour the long-term ambition of vanquishing their opponents. Such a mentality may even persist in the event of a limited peace deal, with multi-party elections being treated not as the catalyst for a new type of democratic politics but rather a continuation of the conflict by other means. As Angola demonstrated in 1992, this scenario is much more likely to arise if elections have not been preceded by lengthy negotiations leading to the creation of a new political and constitutional architecture.[101]

Pretoria has engaged with at least two African conflicts trapped in this zero-sum-game mindset since 1994: in Angola in the mid-1990s, and in Libya in 2011. Its attempts at mediation to encourage a settlement along South African lines foundered on government hostility in the former conflict, and on opposition hostility in the latter. In 1994 the People's Movement for the Liberation of Angola (MPLA) regime, an ally of the ANC, firmly rejected a South African offer to mediate between it and rebel organisation the National Union for the Total Independence of Angola (UNITA).[102] After UNITA refused to accept defeat in the 1992 elections and returned to war, the MPLA saw no scope for further peace talks and rebuffed South African diplomatic overtures in favour of the pursuit of a military victory (which it would finally achieve in 2002).[103] In Libya, South Africa overestimated the potential for successful conflict resolution based upon its preference for establishing a government of national unity (GNU). The Gadhafi regime and its rebel opponents lacked a common sense of nationhood and a willingness to share the political space. At various points in the conflict, the two sides openly acknowledged that they sought the total defeat of their enemy. In contrast to the South African experience, GNU deals are almost impossible to construct in the throes of all-out war, when neither side is prepared to concede at the negotiating table what it has won at considerable cost on the battlefield. In Libya, South Africa was also hampered by the unfortunate precedent of the Zimbabwean national-unity agreement mediated by Mbeki in 2008–09. His so-called Global Political Agreement allowed Mugabe to remain president and the ruling party, ZANU–PF, to retain all key security portfolios, while the opposition, Movement for Democratic Change, was relegated to the status of a junior partner. Having permitted ZANU–PF to retain control of the state apparatus and persist in its attempts to liquidate the opposition, the deal badly damaged hopes that a GNU could pave the way for stability and democratic reform.

Aware of the ANC's historically close ties to the Gadhafi regime,[104] Libyan rebel forces would have suspected that, as in Zimbabwe, a South African-sponsored power-sharing arrangement would essentially be a mechanism to preserve the regime. Therefore, the failure of Pretoria's Libyan diplomacy is at least partly rooted in the partisan posture that it adopted in

Zimbabwe. The danger for South Africa's reputation in Africa is that its instinctive resort to the GNU formula risks antagonising both the incumbent regime and the opposition, who see it as pressurising them to accommodate rebel demands and favouring the government respectively. Angola apart, the common charge levelled at South Africa in these situations is that its conflict-resolution and -mediation initiatives display an overt bias towards existing governments. In Zimbabwe, Côte d'Ivoire, Libya, Sudan and, more recently, Burundi, South Africa has been accused of partisanship and favouritism towards the Mugabe, Gbagbo, Gadhafi, Bashir and Nkurunziza regimes respectively. This perception has destroyed opposition groups' confidence in Pretoria as an even-handed mediator.[105]

Similarly, in the DRC in 2016–17, South Africa failed to energetically press President Joseph Kabila to hold elections, remaining relatively sanguine about the prospect of him remaining in office well beyond December 2016, when his second term officially ended. Indeed, the Zuma government accepted without objection Kabila's implausible reasoning that, due to an outdated electoral roll, elections could not be held in 2017, as agreed in the December 2016 St Sylvestre deal between the government and opposition. Pretoria expressed its support for, and solidarity with, the regime despite the opposition's belief that Kabila had engaged in a deceptive power grab.[106] The instinctive support for incumbent governments was confirmed when Pretoria simultaneously sought to water down any investigation by the UN's Human Rights Council into violence in the DRC's Kasai region of the allegations of extrajudicial killings by the security forces. Instead, South Africa insisted that the AU and the United Nations merely provide technical assistance to the DRC's own internal investigation.[107] The ANC government's statist tendency is particularly pronounced where it has ties to African governments that can be traced back to the liberation era. Thus, South African policy focuses on the need to sustain fellow liberation movements in power, out of fear that their defeat and departure may have a domino effect which will eventually undermine the ANC's political dominance at home.[108]

It is also a concern that South Africa may be promoting a brand of conflict resolution in Africa that is increasingly a caricature of its own peace process. South Africa constructed its post-1994 GNU on solid democratic foundations that gave proper weight to voters' wishes in determining the allocation of cabinet seats, portfolios and the presidency. However, elsewhere, GNUs have rewarded those who refuse to accept electoral defeat and are prepared to hold their country to ransom by threatening (or actually unleashing) violent turmoil unless they are accommodated. In contrast, South Africa's power-sharing arrangement was part of an agreed constitutional package put in place in advance of an election rather than the kind of hastily assembled post-election contrivance that has too often allowed a defeated party to circumvent the popular will. Therefore, Pretoria based its approach to post-election Zimbabwe, Côte d'Ivoire and Kenya on a fundamental misreading of the South African process itself. In these countries, power-sharing was a direct consequence of the ruling party's use of state violence to maintain its dominance of government. South Africa's decision to reward such conduct may have been temporarily expedient, but it also caused long-term damage to the prospects for nurturing a democratic culture in Africa, and for embedding core principles such as an unconditional acceptance of election results and an orderly transition of power. The 2008–09 settlement in Zimbabwe effectively endorsed a coup against a democratically elected party by ZANU–PF, which had scorned even the suggestion that it could or should be displaced by an election.[109] By legitimising the coup, South Africa risked creating an unfortunate precedent and encouraging such behaviour elsewhere, to the dismay of democracy activists across the continent. It is one thing to create a process 'aimed at co-opting the bad guys',[110] as René Lemarchand puts it, but quite another for those 'bad guys' to continue to command state power despite electoral defeat due to their capacity to generate post-electoral violence and mayhem. South Africa's failure to appreciate that crucial distinction risks consolidating authoritarian rule across the continent.[111]

Finally, South Africa's approach to conflict resolution in Africa is likely to generate greater resentment, and thereby become less effective, the further it moves beyond the SADC zone. (As ongoing troubles in the DRC, Lesotho, Swaziland and Zimbabwe demonstrate, there is no guarantee of success even among SADC members.)[112] As it frequently lacks an intimate knowledge of the political dynamics in African states beyond the SADC, the South African government's well-intentioned interventions can lead to floundering and even outright failure. Given its limited bureaucratic capacity and often inadequate knowledge of African conflicts,[113] DIRCO is sometimes unable to sustain successful diplomatic initiatives beyond the SADC zone. Moreover, individual states and sub-regional organisations inevitably resent these encroachments on to their turf. This could be seen in the Nigeria-led Economic Community of West African States' response to South African involvement in Côte d'Ivoire in 2010–11,[114] and in the Economic Community of Central African States' reaction to South African engagement in the Central African Republic in 2013. (In the latter effort, which proved unsuccessful, South Africa failed to effectively consult and liaise with other regional power brokers.)[115] This is not to dismiss South Africa's ability to contribute constructively to conflict resolution in Africa – or to dismiss the GNU option in all circumstances – but rather to suggest that a more nuanced approach may be beneficial. Such an approach would require South Africa to have greater sensitivity to the political complexities of the states in which it seeks to mediate; accept that its own model is not a panacea (and may even impede democratisation); and remain aware of situations in which it would be more prudent to stand aside for other regional players. Pretoria's vainglorious conviction that its model is universally relevant risks antagonising political actors across a broad spectrum of African opinion.

South Africa's contribution

Despite these criticisms, many other African states fail to fully acknowledge South Africa's experience on the continent or the contribution to African progress and wellbeing made by a Pretoria confronting severe domestic challenges.[116] This points to shortfalls in the scope and effectiveness of South African public diplomacy, which has been unable to show the country's continental activities in a more favourable light or to downplay those aspects of its behaviour that overshadow its contributions. South Africa has provided much of the capacity needed to build African institutions (principally the AU, contributing 15% of the organisation's budget);[117] engaged in diplomacy and mediation; conducted disaster and humanitarian relief; encouraged development; and redistributed wealth, particularly via the SACU. Almost imperceptibly, South Africa has also emerged as a major source of development assistance in Africa, an area in which its achievements are comparable to those of traditional donors such as the United Kingdom and France. This is quite an achievement for a relatively small middle-income country that has limited experience in the provision and management of aid programmes, and that lacks the kind of bureaucratic infrastructure used by more established donors. The DRC has been the principal beneficiary of this South African largesse, receiving more than US$1bn between 2001 and 2015[118] – although it is unclear whether Pretoria can sustain this level of development assistance. South Africa has also been active across the continent in post-conflict reconstruction and development, seeking to build human, technical and institutional capacity in African states (see Chapter Three).[119] Although much of this activity may have an instrumentalist character – as a stable Africa aligns with South African security and economic interests – it is of real benefit nonetheless. South Africa's interventions have had mixed success, but it is difficult to argue that Africa would be in a better position without them. For example, the penetration of Africa by South African companies has helped reinvigorate long-dormant economic sectors and refurbish a decaying transport infrastructure, while greatly enhancing financial services and introducing some types of advanced technology, such as mobile phones. The process has also expanded consumer choice and provided a better quality of goods and services, while contributing new capital and bringing more sophisticated production techniques and managerial skills to African economies.[120] Moreover, South Africa has pioneered transnational corridors that seek to promote commerce, industry and development along their routes by attracting foreign investment and boosting inter-state trade – the most advanced of these being the Maputo Development Corridor between South Africa and Mozambique.[121] South Africa also chairs the Presidential Infrastructure Championing Initiative, which is advancing several major infrastructure projects across the continent.

South Africa has also played a crucial role in helping to sustain people beyond its borders. The country is home to at least three million migrants from the SADC zone alone (60% of them Zimbabweans, with migrants from Mozambique and

Lesotho the next-largest groups), who send at least R11.2bn (US$788m) in remittances to their home states annually. The lack of complete data on the number of migrants in South Africa, along with the fact that as much as 68% of remittances are thought to be sent using informal means, makes it difficult to accurately calculate this figure. However, it is clear that South Africa remains a vital regional economic hub in helping migrants feed, educate and otherwise raise their families in their home countries. As households that receive remittances have improved economic and health outcomes, South Africa's contribution to combating poverty and human insecurity in Southern Africa and beyond should not be underestimated.[122]

The country can also take credit from its peacemaking efforts in Burundi, the DRC (even if the internal politics of both states remain fragile and unsatisfactory) and Ethiopia and Eritrea, as well as its role in promoting nuclear non-proliferation in Africa and its partially successful attempts to tackle the continental trade in conflict diamonds through the Kimberley Process.[123] Pretoria has also worked assiduously to build closer links between the AU and the UN as a means of enhancing the former's peace and security capacity,[124] and has been pivotal in attempts to build a continental peace and security architecture. Although this activism may fall short of the reach and influence of an outright hegemon, South Africa certainly remains a leading African state. Overall, the country's significant provision of African public goods is strikingly out of kilter with its image as a self-serving state standing aloof from the continent. Many African states implicitly acknowledged this fact when supporting South Africa's candidacy for a non-permanent seat on the UN Security Council in 2007–08 and 2010–11. During the first of these terms, Pretoria raised the salience of African issues to the point that the council hosted its first ever Summit on Peace and Security in Africa.

Yet South Africa now confronts a dilemma in Africa akin to that faced by the US at the global level. Pretoria's economic, political and military interventions often meet with opposition and hostility, but a more passive approach, or a failure to sustain an intervention throughout the reconstruction phase, is frequently viewed as an unacceptable abdication of its responsibilities as a major power. In these circumstances, it is genuinely difficult to fashion a clear and consistent policy that will mobilise support.[125] Regardless of whether it is deserved, this image problem is undermining South Africa's leadership ambitions in Africa and, accordingly, a global stature intimately tied to its capacity to provide African leadership. This is particularly true at a time when the foreign-policy positions that previously enhanced its global profile – a strong commitment to human rights and a bridge-building role between North and South – have effectively withered away. South Africa seems to have enough power to antagonise and alienate other African states, but not enough to impose its will on them (even if it had the desire to do so). If, as Smith contends, 'image and reputation management are important aspects of modern statecraft',[126] South Africa is hampered by the widespread perception that it is domineering, detached, arrogant and self-interested – views that are often contradictory but remain damaging nonetheless. Erasing such impressions will be a formidable task, given that what will appease one African constituency may incur the wrath of another. Furthermore, due to the scale of South Africa's domestic challenges, and the electoral damage that its socio-economic divisions are finally beginning to inflict on the ANC, Pretoria will place a greater emphasis – in reality, if not in rhetoric – on a 'South Africa first' approach. This, in turn, will create further scope for acrimony and discord with other African states.

CHAPTER THREE

The African Renaissance versus the South African Renaissance?

'The basic truth in politics is that foreign policy begins at home.' – Gerrit Olivier[1]

The inauguration of the Mandela government in 1994 greatly improved South Africa's relationships with other African states, creating numerous opportunities for them to collaborate with one another. The country's new leaders acknowledged both its role in destabilising southern Africa during the apartheid era and the debt of gratitude it owed to neighbouring states, which had helped sustain its liberation struggle. Pretoria also recognised that South Africa's interests were best served by economic development and democratisation in African states, accepting that it had an obligation to act as one of the principal architects of African security and development. Observers always expected that these sentiments would be factored into the South African policymaking process at some level. But it was difficult to quantify how they should be balanced against other priorities, and what this would mean for Pretoria's relationships with African countries outside the Southern African Development Community

(SADC) zone, which were less focused on issues such as destabilisation and the need for South African reciprocity. In addition to the various image problems undermining South Africa's regional diplomatic efforts (see Chapter Two), domestic challenges are likely to overshadow the country's commitments to the continent, further weakening its leadership position.

Two decades into the democratic era, the failure to deliver fundamental socio-economic change is finally beginning to impose serious political costs on the ruling African National Congress (ANC). The sharp fall in support for the party in the August 2016 municipal elections[2] appeared to serve as a warning of things to come. As the pressure of domestic responsibilities rises,[3] South Africa will be forced to scale down its activism elsewhere in Africa, particularly its developmental role.

To date, the government and the ANC have rarely, if ever, publicly acknowledged the tension between domestic and foreign-policy priorities. Indeed, it is too often complacently assumed in government foreign-policy documents that the components of South Africa's foreign policy – including its Southern African and wider continental goals; relationship with the West; role within the BRICS and the Global South; and efforts at global governance – fit seamlessly with its domestic agenda. In reality, attempts to manage such a complex set of relations risk incoherence and disorder. By reducing its continental role, South Africa is likely to antagonise states and peoples in Africa and further afield, given the expectations generated by its long-standing claims to a pivotal role in the promotion of the African Renaissance. Pretoria may regard this outcome as undesirable, but far less problematic than the upheaval that would result from a failure to transform a fractured South African society.

Failure to transform

The greatest threats to South Africa's long-term interests and leadership aspirations on the continent are the structural weaknesses of its economy, widespread poverty in the country and other crippling socio-economic problems that have continued to blight the post-apartheid era. 'Transformation', a government mantra since the birth of democratic South Africa, has proved an elusive concept: too much of the legacy of apartheid remains deeply entrenched. In his May 1994 inaugural address, president Nelson Mandela stated that political emancipation must serve as a catalyst 'to liberate all our people from the continued bondage of poverty, deprivation, suffering, gender and other discrimination'.[4] Indeed, Mandela had made this argument as far back as 1991, saying:

> A simple vote without food, shelter [and] healthcare is to use first-generation rights as a smokescreen to obscure the deep underlying forces which dehumanise people. It is to create an appearance of equality and justice … We do not want freedom without bread, nor do we want bread without freedom.[5]

Thus, South African society's failure to transform will have several domestic and regional political consequences. This is not to argue that the ANC government has entirely failed since 1994, or that South Africa has experienced, in Abegunrin's phrase, 'a revolution without change'.[6] It is useful to recall the observation of Chester Crocker, US assistant secretary of state for African Affairs in the Reagan era, that South Africa often served as 'a magnet for one-dimensional minds'.[7] As a consequence, observers should resist the temptation to either idealise or dismiss the country's successes, when the situation is actually much more complex. The government can point to significant progress in several areas, such as the provision of electricity, clean drinking water, housing and primary health-care. The government has also provided social grants that keep 17 million people out of absolute poverty, even if the level of those benefits remains extremely low and those aged between 18 and 59 have no access to social security.[8] The infant-mortal-ity rate has continued to fall throughout the post-1994 era, reaching 34.4 deaths per 1,000 live births in 2015, compared to 51.2 deaths per 1,000 live births in 2002. The mortality rate among children under the age of five has also fallen, from 77.2 per 1,000 in 2002 to 45.1 per 1,000 in 2015.[9]

However, the country continues to labour under a range of socio-economic problems which, le Pere claims, are collectively producing 'a growing sense of popular despair, cynicism and alienation'[10] among the millions of black South Africans who, as Abegunrin notes, exist outside 'the charmed circles of growth and development'.[11] The unemployment rate, which disproportionately affects black South Africans, stood at 27.7% in January 2017, the highest figure since September 2003. Using a definition of unemployment expanded to include those who wanted to work but were not actively looking for a job – so-called 'discouraged work seekers' – the unemployment rate stood at 36.4%, representing 9.3m people.[12] On either reading, this is one of the highest unemployment rates in the world. Moreover, 73% of the unemployed are under the age of 36.[13] The joblessness rate among those aged 15–24 stood at 49.9% in official figures published in July 2015, and a colossal 63.1% on the expanded definition of unemployment. This problem creates the raw material for social unrest, crime, xenophobia and, ultimately, political volatility. Job creation therefore remains the most urgent issue confronting South Africa.[14] The 2012 National Development Plan (NDP) aims to reduce unemployment to 14% by 2020, but the country is not on course to reach that target and, if anything, is moving in the opposite direction. In terms of poverty, in 2015 the government agency Statistics South Africa found that 21.7% of South Africans – 12m people – lived in absolute poverty, meaning they could not afford to meet their basic nutritional requirements, while 53.8% fell within a broader definition of poverty, surviving on less than R779 (US$61) per month. Thus, the South African government failed to meet its target to eradicate poverty by 2015.[15] Almost one-third of South African children are stunted at an early age due to inadequate access to food, which impedes cognitive and physical development.[16] Depressingly, the percentage of black South Africans living in poverty actually increased by 10% between 1994 and 2014, definitive confirmation of the government's inability to fundamentally transform South African society.[17]

South Africa also remains one of the world's most unequal societies, with inequality as high as it was in 1994. In South Africa, the richest decile of citizens own 65% of the country's wealth; in comparison, the richest decile own 55% and 45% of national wealth in Brazil and the United States respectively.[18] Although the democratic era has witnessed the emergence of a black middle class – a principal beneficiary of the new order[19] – and inequality is now intra- as well as inter-racial, race remains the most reliable indicator of poverty, inequality and life opportunities. The poor are overwhelmingly concentrated in the black African population, while 80% of the richest decile are white.[20] In 1996 the ratio of white per capita income to other races was 3.9:1; in 2014 it was 4.5:1.[21] By 2016, black South Africans had an average income of R2,600 (US$277) per month, compared with their white compatriots' average income of R11,700 (US$795) per month.

Homelessness is exacerbated by the pace of urbanisation in the country: as of August 2013, 3.3m South Africans still lived in shacks or makeshift structures.[22] Despite the resources directed towards it, South Africa's education system remains in deep crisis. With the system turning out too few skilled people, the country continues to languish at the bottom of international educational league tables. For example, in a 2014 World Economic Forum report, South Africa was ranked bottom of 148 states for maths and science, and 146th for the overall quality of its education.[23] As of mid-2016, 6.2m South Africans, or 11% of the population, were HIV positive – although, in one of the relatively few achievements of the Zuma presidency, infection rates and deaths from AIDS are both falling due to a more proactive approach to treatment and prevention. However, the HIV/AIDS pandemic has significantly lowered life expectancy in South Africa, even if this is now beginning to move up again, standing at 60.6 years for males and 64.2 years for females in 2015.[24] The health sector continues to be defined by a stark, and largely racial, polarisation between expensive private services covering 15–20% of South Africans and rudimentary, under-resourced services covering the other 80–85%.[25] Finally, although official statistics show that 92.9% of adults were functionally literate in 2013, the criteria used – an ability to read and write short sentences – set a very low standard for literacy.[26]

Perhaps the most troubling issue is that these daunting challenges must now be addressed within an economy that is near to stagnation, and that generates considerable pessimism across all business sectors.[27] The South African economy's rates of growth have been lethargic at 2.5% in 2013, 1.7% in 2014 and 1.3% in 2015.[28] This fell to 0.3% in 2016, with the IMF forecasting a growth rate of 0.8% for 2017[29] (other organisations forecast an even gloomier 0.2%, due to the political and financial turbulence created by President Jacob Zuma's March 2017 decision to sack his finance minister, Pravin Gordhan).[30] Indeed, the South African economy technically moved into recession with a 0.7% decrease in GDP in the first quarter of 2017, following a 0.3% contraction in the previous quarter.[31] Growth for the 2017–20 period is unlikely to exceed 2–3%,[32] falling far short of the 6–7% growth rates required to bring down unemployment. In fairness to South Africa, these recent figures are not strikingly dissimilar to those for other medium-sized economies like Argentina, Chile and Mexico, although they are poorer than that of its continental peer, Egypt. That said, such weak growth will further increase unemployment, making it difficult for the government to sustain its large-scale provision of social grants. Yet attempting to reduce these grants is fraught with political risk.[33] Following the 2014 general election, ratings agencies came close to downgrading South Africa's sovereign credit rating to non-investment, or 'junk', status, bemoaning the government's incoherence on policy and failure to address the country's structural economic weaknesses.[34] Standard & Poor's and Fitch eventually made these downgrades in April 2017 due to the dismissal of Gordhan, who had established a strong global reputation for economic prudence and was determined to protect the treasury from political interference. Both agencies expressed concern about the country's economic trajectory, particularly the risks posed by populist economic policies, political instability, low growth rates, the condition of many state-owned enterprises (which are rife with cronyism) and the government's management of public finances and lack of commitment to structural reform.[35] Moody's followed with a downgrade of its own in June 2017, citing many of the same concerns – although it did not yet move South Africa to junk status.[36] Amounting to a vote of no confidence in the government's management of the economy, these downgrades have had serious implications for the country's costs of borrowing and ability to attract investment, and thus to strengthen the economy and create jobs.[37] In these straitened circumstances,

Pretoria is also likely to face an intensification of the sometimes violent service-delivery protests that have persisted for several years in many black South African communities,[38] as well as a heightened prospect of strikes in South Africa's always volatile industrial sector.

Implications of the failure to transform for Africa policy

This failure to transform South African society – as opposed to merely ameliorating some of its worst problems – is affecting South Africa's ability to provide African leadership and project its influence across the continent. The adverse effects on the relationship with Africa are especially apparent in two areas. Firstly, South Africa's ability to portray itself as a champion of the marginalised and a scourge of global poverty has been severely compromised by the fact that, a quarter of a century on from liberation, its own society remains deeply polarised by poverty and inequality. The failure to achieve socio-economic transformation has diminished South Africa's weight and moral authority in the African diplomatic conversation, puncturing its aura of inspiration. South Africa's soft power, strength of example and excoriations of 'global apartheid' will count for little in Africa while it maintains the apartheid-era's legacy of income inequality and social deprivation at home.

Secondly, although the Department of International Relations and Cooperation (DIRCO) is certain to maintain its official line that 'Africa will remain at the core of all our foreign policy endeavours',[39] the political challenge posed by severe socio-economic deficits will necessitate a shift towards a narrower focus on domestic change and away from deep, sustained engagement with wider Africa – unless this engagement has obvious domestic benefits. Were it to persist with its extensive commitments to Africa (see Chapter Two), Pretoria would risk triggering a domestic backlash by creating the impression that the government is prioritising African interests over those of South Africans. The ANC once existed in a political comfort zone sustained by its heroic image and liberation credentials, in which a strong reaffirmation of its continental obligations and 'progressive internationalist' mission may have been relatively cost-free. However, the party is now in more treacherous political territory, as the reserves of voter loyalty accumulated during the apartheid era no longer appear to be inexhaustible. In the August 2016 local-government elections, the ANC achieved its worst result of the democratic era, gaining just 54% of the vote and losing major strongholds in Nelson Mandela Bay, Pretoria and Johannesburg. The results appeared to signal the end of an era in which the party had defied the laws of political gravity, consistently winning elections by huge margins despite its patchy performance in government.[40] Although the ANC's share of the vote has declined at each election under Zuma since 2009, the municipal elections of August 2016 confirmed a trend in which the party is haemorrhaging support in urban areas, becoming increasingly reliant on support in more conservative rural areas. In a country experiencing a rapid rate of urbanisation, this trend points to long-term decline, with the ANC becoming over-reliant upon a shrinking demographic. For the first time, South Africa has entered into an era of genuinely competitive multi-party politics: the ANC's opponents have opportunities to further erode its dominance in 2019 and to end it altogether by 2024.[41]

This raises long-deferred questions about how the ANC should respond to electoral threats.[42] Assuming that its response remains confined within constitutional parameters, these intensifying pressures are creating a climate that will obligate the ANC to focus on the domestic political economy as a matter of self-interest – indeed, survival. Hitherto, there has been a casual assumption in ANC and government discussion documents that the objectives of domestic transformation and the creation of a better Africa dovetail with each other.[43] This is wishful thinking. In an era of growing resource constraints, urgent domestic priorities and meaningful political competition, there is an underlying tension between these two objectives; effectively addressing both lies beyond South Africa's limited capabilities. Confronting what Chris Alden and Garth le Pere call South Africa's own 'horsemen of the apocalypse' – poverty, unemployment and inequality[44] – is certain to deflect attention from the African agenda rather than complement it. In a context of such acute social needs, it is difficult to see how South Africa can build a 'moral economy', as they put it.[45] This type of economy would address domestic needs and embrace a progressive, development-oriented Africa policy rather than trading them off against each other. In fact, despite their abstract appeal, concepts such as partnership and balanced and equitable development – as well as efforts to rein in a supposedly predatory South African corporate sector – are likely to become casualties of Pretoria's imperative to address domestic issues. Abegunrin's hope that South Africa can harness its power and technological advancement to 'become to Africa what Japan has been to the Pacific Basin, the dynamo that energizes and drives those economically underdeveloped countries to become economically viable',[46] appears to be increasingly an unrealistic and remote prospect.

Here, South Africa finds itself trapped in yet another paradoxical situation. The lack of domestic transformation is the single largest security challenge facing the country and the most significant threat to the ANC government's political prospects. It is also a major barrier to South Africa retaining its legitimacy and leadership role on the continent. However, the need to pursue transformation and placate domestic constituencies requires a level of insularity and prioritisation that is likely to undermine any ambitions of regional leadership. Ultimately, delivering domestic socio-economic progress is the South African government's primary responsibility, without which faith in democracy may wither. Therefore, the principal (though not sole) purpose of South African foreign policy should be what Mzukisi Qobo and Memory Dube describe as the 'grounding of foreign policy goals within a domestic development strategy',[47] and the creation of an external climate that will help the government realise its domestic objectives.

The 2012 NDP explicitly states that foreign policy should be firmly anchored in the domestic agenda of eradicating poverty, creating jobs and reducing inequality – thereby inferring that the two had been insufficiently integrated with each other in the past. Although president Thabo Mbeki had a grand strategic vision for Africa that required the construction of a new continental architecture, Cilliers, Schünemann and Moyer note that all too often it appeared that he 'prioritised external engagement over domestic development'.[48] This approach had limited appeal in a country with such pressing social problems and one whose citizens appeared to lack great enthusiasm for the cause of Africa. Mbeki's image as a foreign-policy president was markedly out of step with the priorities of the South African population, as measured by opinion polls that, unsurprisingly, showed South Africans' principal concern to be domestic transformation. According to these surveys, a large majority of people criticised Mbeki for spending too much time abroad, and for devoting too much time, energy and resources to African conflicts rather than South Africa's problems.[49] This reinforced the impression that he was out of touch with South Africa's political reality, a perception which undermined his position both inside and outside the ruling party.[50] Ultimately, any state seeking to sustain a leadership role beyond its borders requires 'a stable source of domestic political support'[51] – without which its economic, diplomatic or military interventions will lack legitimacy and staying power. Unless the ANC government can persuade its domestic constituencies that an interventionist Africa policy can help facilitate domestic progress, popular support for extensive and protracted external engagements is likely to melt away. The Zuma administration recognised this in 2009, when Ibrahim Ibrahim, DIRCO's deputy minister, said that foreign policy would now be 'driven by the need to deliver to the masses of our people, which is at the core of our national interest'.[52]

However, the persistence of the socio-economic problems mapped out above suggests that the government has failed to ground foreign policy in domestic concerns to any significant degree, perhaps because of a lack of political pressure to do so. However, the situation changed in the aftermath of the 2016 municipal elections, and Nelson Mandela's 1993 statement that an incoming ANC government would 'resist any pressure or temptation to pursue its own interests at the expense of the sub-continent'[53] now appears to reflect a ritualistic position, an essential part of foreign-policy rhetoric but an inaccurate guide to actual policy behaviour. Given the scale of South Africa's domestic challenges – and the pressure on the ANC to demonstrate progress in addressing them – the country's economic diplomacy now seems likely to become a more hard-nosed and self-interested affair, crowding out other considerations and leaving South Africa exposed to renewed accusations of ruthless mercantilism.

Turning inwards is also likely to damage the ANC's image of itself, and its aspirations for South Africa to be a state deeply rooted in, what Brendan Vickers has labelled, the 'politics of solidarity'.[54] However, pan-African solidarity may have limited influence on the daily formulation of policy when the ANC considers its own vital self-interests to be at stake. The familiar argument that the South African interest is best served by stabilising the continent may be intellectually unassailable but it is politically weak and difficult to advance against a backdrop of domestic poverty, chronically high unemployment and inadequate public services. Consequently, beyond the confines of the country's black African intelligentsia, 'South Africa first' sentiments remain strong – the xenophobic attacks highlighted in Chapter Two are but one manifestation of this – and are likely to eclipse more esoteric concerns with the African agenda, pan-African solidarity and anti-imperialism. The ANC leadership may see itself as fully committed to the cause of Africa, despite its attempts to impose tighter visa restrictions on foreign Africans attempting to enter South Africa[55] and its inadequate response to the xenophobic attacks. But this perspective is hard to reconcile with many South Africans, hostility towards peacekeeping, development assistance or the presence of foreign Africans in South Africa.[56]

Thus, Pretoria lacks the domestic base needed to sustain the more burdensome aspects of hegemony, with most South Africans viewing the difficulties of other states in the region as rather disconnected from their own immediate problems. Moreover, although South Africa routinely acknowledges that regional development is in its own best interests,[57] this does not mean that the country can or should immediately pursue such development, or that it has the responsibility or capacity to do so.

To a significant degree, South Africa has been hoisted by its own petard. The country's rhetoric on the African Renaissance has set it up for failure by fuelling unrealistic expectations about the role it might play on the continent. To retreat from that now is to invite ridicule and disdain for over-promising and under-delivering, the essence of a weak foreign policy. Yet, as Maxi Schoeman notes, South Africa cannot afford to become an all-purpose firefighter, problem solver and benefactor for Africa as 'leadership attention, resources and energy will have to be expended at home, not abroad'.[58] Indeed, given the enormity of its domestic challenges, the country will struggle to sustain existing commitments, let alone supplement them. Some analysts, such as Happy Kayuni and Richard Tambulasi, have argued that the most effective way for South Africa to help Africa is by putting its own house in order. Success there will have a demonstration effect, causing others to seek to emulate the South African experience.[59] Until it does, they argue, the state will be incapable of constructing a 'consensual hegemony' in Africa.[60] This seems an overly sanguine assessment because it ignores the fact that many African states are incapable of emulating South African levels of economic development. More crucially, the danger is that any policy driven by a much narrower pursuit of South African self-interest in Africa via trade, market expansion and investment will further extend its already considerable economic dominance over most African states, thereby generating increased hostility towards the country. This approach is likely to draw criticism that the country is once again paying lip service to African solidarity while effectively exploiting and neglecting Africa. As there are likely to be no cost-free options for South Africa in this situation, it is unrealistic to believe that the country can prioritise its own development – and the self-interested policies that inevitably flow from this – without further contaminating its relationships with other African states. In the harsher political climate that the ANC government has entered, it has become apparent that the deferral of difficult choices – hitherto the modus operandi of the Zuma administration – is likely to exact an increasing price for South Africa.

Rise of Nigeria

Therefore, despite its strength relative to its neighbours, South Africa may now lack the base to launch extensive engagements in Africa. Although the country can hardly be viewed as a global economic power – with the world's 33rd-largest economy,[61] and accounting for a mere 0.5% of global trade[62] – it has long been influential on the continent. South Africa is a major power in the Southern African Customs Union (SACU) and an economic hegemon in the SADC. As South Africa accounts for almost 70% of the SADC zone's GDP and 60% of its trade,[63] the sub-region's states are 'cast in a hub and spoke relationship to South Africa'.[64] The country is an important economic actor, albeit not a hegemon, in Africa beyond the SADC, but its material power in this region is declining. South Africa's economy may still be 40 times larger than that of the average sub-Saharan African state, but its share of sub-Saharan African GDP has declined from 50% in 1994 to 25% in 2013.[65] Moreover, South Africa's previous levels of dominance were always less a display of its own innate strength than of the dysfunctional nature of most post-independence African states.

The event that best symbolised the end of South African dominance came in April 2014, when the Nigerian economy supplanted that of South Africa as the continent's largest. This forced a reappraisal of African states' power and leadership capabilities among members of the international community – not least the BRICS group, which had admitted South Africa three years earlier as a means of enhancing its credibility in Africa. Moreover, Nigeria's economy is projected by the International Futures Base Case forecasts for the period 2015–40 to account for almost 3% of the global economy by 2040, and to grow considerably faster than South Africa's between now and then.[66] Nigeria's rise – along with that of other emerging African powers, such as Angola, Ethiopia, Kenya and Ghana

– also challenges Pretoria's established narrative that South Africa automatically serves as the gateway to Africa for external investors looking to explore opportunities on the continent.[67]

However, while the importance of Nigeria's economic rise should not be underestimated, it is also important to remain sensitive to the country's considerable weaknesses vis-à-vis South Africa. The Nigerian economy is highly reliant on the oil sector, with the government drawing 80% of its revenue from the product. Equally, while South Africa's problems with corruption have escalated since the Mandela era – particularly under Zuma[68] – they are still far less acute than those of Nigeria, which is consistently ranked in the bottom fifth of Transparency International's annual Corruption Perceptions Index. Indeed, out of the 176 states on the 2016 index, the countries placed 63rd and 136th respectively.[69] Unlike South Africa, Nigeria suffers from pronounced ethnic and religious divisions, and is currently in the throes of brutal sectarian conflict with the insurgent group Boko Haram. Before the inauguration of Muhammadu Buhari as president in 2015, the Nigerian state appeared unable to address the challenge posed by the group. Furthermore, 60% of Nigerians lived in absolute poverty[70] and 70% on less than ten rand per day.[71] By 2015, Nigeria's per capita GDP was US$2,178, well below South Africa's US$5,274 (Nigeria's population is 186m, while South Africa's is 56m).[72] In 2015 the United Nations placed Nigeria at 152nd and South Africa at 116th out of the 188 states on its Human Development Index, categorising the former as in the 'low human development' category and the latter as in the 'medium human development' category.[73]

Nigeria has suffered a protracted crisis of governance in the independence era, spending 33 years under the rule of failing military regimes and the remainder governed by civilian administrations routinely mired in corruption and underachievement. With Boko Haram the latest manifestation of what Cilliers, Schünemann and Moyer call a 'wider political economy of violence',[74] this dysfunction has undermined Nigeria's stability and international standing,[75] and is certain to shape the perceptions of external investors despite the attention generated by the country's recent economic advances. Although South Africa's economic problems are serious and debilitating, the country has advantages over Nigeria that lend it greater global status and influence, such as political stability and the absence of civil conflict, as well as established democratic institutions and a robust constitution. In the 2015 Ibrahim Index – which measures the quality of African governance based on the criteria of safety and security; political participation and human rights; human development; and economic opportunity – South Africa placed fourth, and Nigeria 39th, out of 54 states.[76] In comparison to Nigeria, South Africa has greater access to advanced technology, higher levels of industrialisation and economic diversity, and a larger financial sector, with the Johannesburg Stock Exchange the eighteenth-largest exchange in the world as of 2015.[77] South Africa also has a more impressive transport infrastructure and a better sovereign credit rating, despite the downgrades in the Zuma era.[78] This all suggests that South Africa can remain Africa's most developed, industrialised and advanced economy – if not its largest. In October 2016, the IMF still placed the Nigerian economy ahead of South Africa's as the continent's largest.[79] Much depends on the quality of South African leadership and its economic acumen, an area in which its recent record is, at best, undistinguished. Nonetheless, Nigeria's development will also provide lucrative opportunities for South African companies. It has long been axiomatic among South African politicians and commentators that development throughout the continent – but especially in a country as large as Nigeria, which can make such a major contribution to African wellbeing – is in the interests of the entire continent.[80] Ideally, capable and imaginative leadership – hardly a guaranteed outcome in either state – will help establish a constructive Nigeria–South Africa relationship, facilitating burden-sharing and advancing African interests without recourse to a vain, self-defeating pursuit of pre-eminence.

A diminished South African role?

There were signs that South Africa would take on a more circumspect role in African development even before the country's August 2016 municipal elections; the ANC's poor results in the contest will lend further impetus to this shift. The trend of declining engagement is evident in two principal areas: post-conflict reconstruction and development (PCRD), and financial commitment to the SACU.

South Africa is actively involved in conflict prevention, peacekeeping and PCRD.[81] As Savo Heleta argues, the purpose of PCRD is 'to create a stable environment, consolidate lasting peace and prevent the return of violent conflict in the future',[82] a process that he recognises is likely to be 'intricate and long'.[83] Much of South Africa's PCRD activity in African states recovering from protracted periods of violence and social breakdown – such as South Sudan – has involved not direct payments but attempts to build institutions, strengthen governance mechanisms, provide technical assistance, organise elections and train personnel, such as civil servants.[84] This activity involves a range of government departments, as well as state-owned enterprises and state agencies such as the Development Bank of Southern Africa, the Industrial Development Corporation, the Independent Electoral Commission and the Human Sciences Research Council. (Pretoria sometimes involves the defence department in these undertakings, a practice that Heleta views as a dangerous blurring of the demarcation line between military activity and developmental work.)[85]

This array of projects across different departments and agencies is difficult to coordinate, making for incoherent policy and challenges in accurately measuring PCRD expenditure. The government could mitigate these problems by operationalising the South African Development Partnership Agency (SADPA), bringing all related activities under the remit of one institution. Disbursements to the continent via the African Renaissance Fund – through which many of South Africa's PCRD initiatives are funded (alongside a variety of other measures such as conflict prevention and emergency relief programmes), and which SADPA will eventually replace – totalled R199m (US$13.8m) in 2016, down from R208m (US$14.5m) the previous year.[86]

However, South Africa's capacity to encourage best practice in these areas is limited by neo-patrimonial leadership in many African states. These states are prepared to observe some of the rituals, procedures and outward forms of good governance, so long as they do not encroach upon the real centres of power and the parallel structures that preserve the flow of resources between patron and client. South Africa's record of confronting such systems has been unimpressive and – in line with Pretoria's shift away from promoting democracy and human rights abroad (see Chapter One) – has been characterised by denial, obfuscation and, at times, ignorance.

This lacklustre approach to the continent appears to reflect a lack of good governance in South Africa itself, under Zuma's incompetent and directionless administration. Systemic corruption undermines the state's capacity to act by diverting funds intended for crucial domestic and foreign projects into the hands of predatory elites. Graft further increases the strain placed on PCRD resources by the government's need to refocus on domestic priorities. For example, at the February 2014 African Solidarity Conference in Addis Ababa, an event held to mobilise funding for PCRD, President Zuma reaffirmed South Africa's commitment to the effort but, unlike Nigerian and Algerian leaders, did not pledge any new funds to it.[87] In Burundi, Lesotho, the Democratic Republic of the Congo (DRC) and South Sudan, Pretoria has engaged in at least some of the three phases of PCRD: short-term emergency action, medium-term transitional activity and longer-term development programmes. These phases involve a range of activities, including electoral organisation, peacekeeping, the establishment of tax-raising processes, the consolidation of peace agreements, reconciliation and efforts to address the root causes of conflict.[88] Were it not for its other commitments, South Africa might make a persuasive case for its involvement in all aspects of the PCRD role, particularly given that the AU's embryonic structures in this area lack the capacity for complex, multifaceted operations. However, the stabilisation of post-conflict societies is never a quick fix, and will require an open-ended, long-term commitment. As Cheryl Hendricks and Amanda Lucey state:

> If [South Africa] is to be a credible player in the fields of post-conflict development and peacebuilding, it will have to come up with a comprehensive strategy, develop the necessary human resource capacity, provide adequate financial resources and be prepared to be in post-conflict countries for extensive periods of time.[89]

This undertaking would require a level of engagement that lies well beyond South Africa's current capabilities, given the country's domestic socio-economic challenges, particularly the constraints imposed by its underperforming economy. Thus, efforts to become a 'credible player' in Africa would come at too high a price domestically. To stake out a more modest and achievable role, Pretoria could seek to pre-empt and deflect criticism of its position by largely confining its PCRD efforts to SADC states such as Angola, the DRC and Mozambique, where it can make a more informed and effective contribution. Elsewhere in Africa, Pretoria could find a niche suited to its expertise – such as advice on reconciliation processes or constitutional design – as part of a multilateral PCRD process in which other African states take the lead.

Since 1994, one of the most glaring weaknesses of South Africa's public diplomacy in Africa has been the country's failure to widely publicise its generosity as an aid donor – even if, for presentational reasons, it prefers to couch this generosity in terms such as 'development assistance' and 'development partnership'. South Africa has comfortably exceeded the UN benchmark of spending 0.7% of GDP on development assistance, a highly impressive feat for a developing state with formidable socio-economic problems.[90] If financial transfers within the SACU – amounting to 4.5% of GDP by 2013 according to some reports – are factored in, South Africa has a strong claim to being the most generous aid donor in the world.[91] South Africa may have failed to draw the plaudits its generosity deserves because it makes most of these transfers to a small group of countries: Botswana, Lesotho, Namibia and Swaziland (BLNS). The SACU agreement already favoured the BLNS group in its original 1969 incarnation, but became even more generous in revenue distribution towards these states after it was revised in 2002. Under the deal, South Africa contributes around 97%, but receives only 17%, of the SACU customs revenue pool.[92] In 2014–15, South Africa unconditionally paid out R51.7billion

(US$4.8bn) – more than 5% of its tax revenue – to the BLNS group out of a total revenue pool of R80bn (US$7.4bn). These transfers accounted for 50% of government revenue in Swaziland, 44% in Lesotho, 35% in Namibia and 30% in Botswana, reflecting these states' unhealthy dependency on South Africa.[93] However, the South African government has been dissatisfied with this arrangement for some time. The treasury considers such a lop-sided arrangement to be unsustainable given South Africa's domestic development needs – not least because Botswana has a higher per capita GDP than South Africa[94] and the transfers allow the BLNS group to set lower personal and corporate tax rates, thereby competing with South Africa for investment.[95]

In many ways, the SACU situation is emblematic of the difficulties South Africa is likely to encounter as it seeks to scale down its African commitments. By suddenly or unilaterally reducing financial transfers under SACU, Pretoria would flout its regional commitments and risk triggering financial instability, if not implosion, in Swaziland and Lesotho (while creating significant challenges for Botswana and Namibia). Accordingly, these states would be forced to reduce spending on education, health and other public services. South Africa must be careful that justified adjustment of an unbalanced relationship does not lead to economic breakdown, insecurity or state failure among its neighbours, which would increase the flow of refugees into South Africa.[96] Although efforts to fundamentally reshape the SACU arrangement may take a decade, Pretoria is likely to press for an early review of the revenue-sharing process, with the aim of allocating resources more equitably and gradually reducing the BLNS group's dependence on South Africa. Pretoria also aims to move away from general revenue transfers and towards an arrangement in which other SACU countries would draw funding from the revenue pool by submitting plans for specific development projects. These states would likely resist such a move, perceiving it as South Africa's crude attempt to assert its dominance by vetting their development agendas (particularly if development assistance to Swaziland and Lesotho is explicitly tied to political reform). Yet, faced with its own pressing domestic development problems, South Africa can no longer afford – if it ever could – to expend such a vast amount on sustaining an obsolete and unhealthy arrangement.

What can South Africa do?

None of this is to suggest that South Africa should entirely disengage from broader African affairs. This would be neither practical nor desirable for the country. Instead, the challenge is to find a way to meet its African responsibilities and contribute effectively to continental development while pursuing domestic socio-economic objectives. South Africa can achieve this as the designated lead state for infrastructural programmes within the New Partnership for Africa's Development (NEPAD), by providing development assistance through the proposed SADPA and by engaging with ventures such as trilateral development cooperation (TDC). However, in each area Pretoria will have to work with restricted budgets, necessitating a more selective assistance programme that may draw criticism for falling short of the extravagant South African rhetoric of the past.

Leaders in Pretoria first floated the idea of SADPA in 2007, but cabinet did not approve the agency until 2009. The Zuma administration intends the SADPA to have an annual budget of R500m (US$34m) and to replace the African Renaissance Fund set up by the Mbeki government. However, despite le Pere's statement that, by 2013, 'all legal, technical and institutional processes had been completed for the Agency's formal establishment',[97] as of late 2017 efforts to establish it remained bogged down in complex bureaucratic processes and 'turf wars' involving DIRCO, the treasury, the Department of Trade and Industry and the president's office.[98] Moreover, parliament, while it is likely to approve SADPA when it finally comes before it, still needs to be fully convinced that the agency can make a vital contribution to development and avoid duplicating the work of other organisations.[99] The delays and prevarication over SADPA's formation are a microcosm of South African policymaking under the Zuma administration, which has repeatedly launched projects with considerable fanfare only to watch them wither on the vine due to endless deferral and a lack of leadership (the 2012 NDP is another such project). If it is established, SADPA will be situated within DIRCO. Thus far, discussions on establishing the agency have perhaps been too fixated on the process of bureaucratic restructuring this will entail, paying too little attention to the financial and capacity constraints within which the agency will have to operate. Like the debate on the SACU, the discussion on development assistance through SADPA's Partnership Development Fund is likely to become more discerning and selective, focusing on the merits of projects that will be monitored to ensure value for money and domestic benefits – behaviour perhaps more akin to that of the traditional Western donors than of South African governments in the post-1994 era.[100]

Lesley Masters maintains that there is still an impressive level of domestic popular support for South African development assistance.[101] Yet Helen Yanacopulos highlights how the public discussion on South Africa's role as a development partner in Africa is muted almost to the point of non-existence. This stands in sharp contrast to the energetic discussion about national development goals, and to international discussions on South Africa's development role on the continent.[102] Yanacopulos notes that 'the state has had to be circumspect about how it presents its international aspirations domestically',[103] which suggests it lacks confidence that it can make a persuasive argument on the provision of development assistance to Africa at a time of urgent need at home. Consequently, Pretoria's development assistance to Africa almost has the feel of a covert operation, something to be smuggled past the South African population to avoid exposing the levels of public support for such initiatives (a situation by no means unique to South Africa). As a consequence, the South African government is more vocal in explaining the rationale for SADPA to external audiences. Proceeding by stealth domestically seems a weak basis on which to sustain long-term African commitments, but in the circumstances this may be the most pragmatic option available.

One way in which South Africa can continue to be an actor in the developmental field without incurring huge costs is through TDC, which involves pivotal Southern states or emerging donors such as South Africa working with established (mainly Western) donors to provide assistance to a third party or beneficiary state. South Africa has already engaged in several TDC projects, including those involving police-training assistance and capacity-building in the DRC and Rwanda, alongside Japan and Sweden respectively. Pretoria has also worked with Germany on a range of programmes and with the US in South Sudan, Mozambique, Namibia and Botswana. TDC has also facilitated South–South cooperation: South Africa has worked with Cuba to provide doctors in Sierra Leone and to support post-conflict reconstruction in Guinea-Bissau; it has worked with Vietnam in assisting farmers in Guinea; and in the India–Brazil–South Africa forum, Pretoria has partnered with its co-members to support schemes in agriculture, environment, science and technology, and social development across Africa.[104] In this way, TDC can help maintain South Africa's development profile on the continent – but it also has several potential dangers. States such as South Africa must be careful not to become – or be perceived as becoming – convenient pawns through which Western states advance their agendas and reinforce the existing global hierarchy. At the same time, South Africa cannot risk destroying its relationship with these established donors, or allowing beneficiary states to be viewed as purely passive recipients of South African generosity. As Masters notes, TDC theoretically offers South Africa an opportunity to return to a modest bridge-building role between the developed and developing worlds, and to avoid having to align itself with either the West or the Global South.[105] However, this is complicated by the fact that, since the Mbeki era, South Africa has unambiguously sought to position itself in global politics as a distinctively African state that uses wider solidarity with developing countries as a leitmotif of its foreign policy. It will be impossible for Pretoria to now abandon that stance and reposition itself as an intermediary or 'neutral broker';[106] at the very least, it will seek to be an advocate for African states. Managing these diverse relationships will require a level of political agility and finesse that could test South African diplomatic capacity – particularly in light of concerns that many officials in DIRCO (among other departments) were appointed or 'deployed' not for their ability but for their loyalty to the ANC.[107] Nonetheless, TDC allows South Africa to remain an active participant in African development programmes without bearing a disproportionate share of the costs. Whether African states will view TDC so benignly, or dismiss it as a token exercise, remains to be seen.

Although democratic South Africa has been reluctant to use its economic weight in Africa as political leverage, its future opportunities to do so will greatly diminish in any case. As Alden and Schoeman observe, the weakness of the country's economy and a range of domestic socio-economic problems will restrict its ability to 'pursue ambitious foreign policy goals even though these goals, are at least, on paper, aligned with its domestic needs and interests'.[108]

South Africa's key dilemma is that it is unable to play an expansive and progressive role on the continent without building a successful and prosperous democracy at home – one that rigorously tackles the social and economic legacy of apartheid. Without an effective domestic policy, Pretoria will lack the economic strength and credibility to undertake any kind of ambitious continental role. Yet the effort to build a healthy society requires a greater inward focus, and accordingly a reduction of African commitments that lack clear domestic benefits. This approach seems likely to re-ignite the African resentments and hostilities towards South Africa that have long simmered just below the surface. Skilful public diplomacy that highlights South Africa's many contributions across the continent may help mitigate the backlash. But should such efforts continue to fail, Pretoria may be forced to accept African opprobrium as the necessary price of addressing its domestic challenges. Of course, given the incompetence, corruption and cronyism now rife in the ANC, something candidly acknowledged by some of the movement's own stalwarts,[109] the government is not guaranteed to succeed in pursuing its domestic agenda even if it decides to de-emphasise regional policy. But the advice offered by Graham Evans in 1999 retains a powerful relevance for contemporary South African leaders:

> The inescapable priority for South Africa at this stage in its development is a foreign policy which reflects the need for domestic reconstruction and economic growth allied to internal political stability. As such, it badly needs an approach that is affordable, supportable and in the best interests of the country as a whole.

Setting the outside world to rights ought to be a sequel not a prologue to setting the inside world to rights. This mitigates against heroic international postures.[110]

CHAPTER FOUR

The plight of the South African National Defence Force

In 1994 the national interest and moral imperatives appeared to have neatly converged to place the promotion of peace and stability in Africa at the centre of South African foreign policy. Due to its economic, military and diplomatic weight relative to other states on the continent, South Africa was widely expected to play a leading role across the entire spectrum of African conflict management. In its first three years, the Mandela government largely focused on domestic issues, including the complex, time-consuming process of integrating the opposing forces of the apartheid era into a new military. At the time, the armed forces lacked experience of peace operations and the defence department faced priority-driven budget cuts that reduced their capacity to act. Furthermore, eager to avoid evoking memories of its apartheid-era policy of destabilisation, South Africa was reluctant to engage in military operations beyond its borders. In 1997, following the creation of the South African National Defence Force (SANDF), then-deputy foreign minister Aziz Pahad stated that South Africa was 'now prepared to play a more forceful role in peacekeeping in Africa'. But, at the same time, the foreign ministry stated:

> Because of our past experience and fear of being
> accused of maintaining a 'big brother' syndrome, we
> did not see ourselves as playing a leading role in the
> region, but now we have come to understand that
> there is an expectation from Africa and the rest of the
> world that we have a role to play.[1]

This process accelerated during Thabo Mbeki's 1999–2008 tenure as president, allowing South African forces to acquire significant experience in peace-support operations on the continent.[2] With Western countries reducing their direct role in African peacekeeping from the late 1990s onwards, and with the growing support for the idea of 'African solutions to African problems', it was commonly believed that the well-regarded SANDF would use its capacity for force projection on the continent, particularly as efforts to build an African security architecture were in their early stages. Since then, South Africa's regional role has continued to expand. When Mandela left office, South Africa had no peacekeeping presence in Africa; by May 2008, more than 3,000 of the country's troops were deployed on missions in Eritrea–Ethiopia, Burundi, the Democratic Republic of the Congo (DRC) and Sudan.[3] South Africa was also making a significant contribution to the development of the African Union's proposed African Standby Force (ASF), providing most of the financial and logistical support for the latter organisation's Southern African Development Community (SADC) Brigade. In a speech to the National Assembly in 2011, Lindiwe Sisulu, then defence minister, made a strong commitment to military deployments across the continent, declaring that the SANDF's presence was vital in preventing a 'degeneration into total anarchy' and was in South Africa's best interests 'economically, politically, morally and socially'.[4]

As the 2012 White Paper on South African participation in peace missions noted, Pretoria had come to embrace preventive diplomacy and the disarmament, demobilisation and reintegration of combatants, as well as peacekeeping and post-conflict reconstruction and development, including security-sector reform.[5] South Africa was also willing, where necessary, to become involved in peace-enforcement activities including the protection of civilian populations, the creation of aid corridors and direct involvement in combat against those deemed to be 'spoilers'. This broad array of tasks required South Africa to coordinate its military operations with unilateral and multilateral development efforts. Although the SANDF has been praised by defence analysts for its ability to perform these tasks within tight budgetary constraints,[6] the force is unlikely to be able to continue to cope with such a complex mixture of responsibilities even if it works in collaboration with multilateral organisations and other African states.

A country's capacity to project military force stands at the heart of any hegemonic project (see Introduction). Although Karen Smith is correct to point out that the use of military power can undermine a state's leadership potential, this is more likely to be the case if it uses force excessively and outside of established multilateral frameworks, or, in a conflict, before making a meaningful attempt to seek peace through diplomatic means. South Africa has generally been careful to situate its interventions within such frameworks, only finding itself in difficulty in this area when its mandate has been vague or confused – as was the case in the Central African Republic (CAR) in 2013. However, the core issue raised by the *South African Defence Review 2014* is South Africa's inability to continue to project military power and to maintain its existing capabilities due to budgetary restrictions. As such, South Africa might be considered a military hegemon within the SADC zone – albeit one reluctant to engage in coercive diplomacy – and an influential power elsewhere on the continent. Nonetheless, the clear message of the review is that the country's military status is in jeopardy due to the SANDF's lack of resources and operational readiness. Unless Pretoria addresses the situation through the remedial action recommended in the review, South Africa's military profile will enter a period of decline that will kill off the country's ambitions of continental leadership.

Conflict in Africa

Westerners' views of African development and conflict resolution have generally become more positive in the twenty-first century, a mood captured by the so-called 'Africa Rising' thesis – with even *The Economist* retreating from its blanket pessimism about Africa's future.[7] Although this is a welcome departure from one-dimensional narratives of African failure, the security problems confronting the continent should not be underestimated. Africa's complex security environment remains prone to conflict due to a wide variety of factors, including ethnic and religious divisions; separatist tendencies; central governments' marginalisation of some communities; and the tensions generated by both resource scarcity and resource abundance – the so-called 'resource curse'. The weakness and dysfunction of states characterised by poor governance, poverty and endemic corruption are also factors. According to the United Nations' 2015 Human Development Index, 37 of 44 states classed as having 'low human development', and the 17 lowest-placed states on the list, are African.[8] These figures provide a sobering reminder of the difficulties that lie ahead: as successive UN secretaries-general have made clear, such levels of underdevelopment act as a catalyst for state failure and, ultimately, conflict.

Most recent African conflicts have been intra-state in character (with the notable exception of the Ethiopia–Eritrea war at the turn of the century). However, intra-state conflicts often transcend national borders, threatening the stability and wellbeing of neighbouring states and even entire sub-regions – as seen in the Boko Haram, Lord's Resistance Army and al-Shabaab insurgencies. At a minimum, these conflicts have disrupted trade; at worst, they have killed large numbers of people, destabilised governments and forced thousands of people to flee to neighbouring states. Intra-state conflicts can also draw in other countries on the side of one of the belligerents, potentially creating a wider conflagration. This effect could be seen from 1998 onwards in the war in the DRC, which drew in Angola, Namibia and Zimbabwe on the side of president Laurent-Désiré Kabila's regime and Uganda and Rwanda on the side of his rebel opponents. As stated in the *South African Defence Review 2014*, post-Cold War African conflicts create 'complex, highly fluid and often lethal environments'.[9] Fragmented and labyrinthine, they involve a range of state and non-state actors with shifting allegiances, have few identifiable frontlines and entrench violence as a form of political exchange, particularly through the routine abuse of civilians. All forms of external intervention are hazardous in these circumstances, as rebel groups are often well armed, experienced and fighting on home turf, while external actors frequently struggle with overextended supply lines and unfamiliar physical and human terrain. Successful engagement with such conflicts requires operational flexibility and an adjustment of orthodox military doctrines that have been shaped by decades of planning for inter-state conflicts. For example, South Africa's arms procurements in the late 1990s focused on enhancing its capabilities for inter-state warfare, and, as a consequence, did little to help the SANDF adapt to this new security environment.[10]

However, the type of conflicts South Africa is likely to face in contemporary African theatres will require a greater emphasis on helicopters, transportable assets, advanced airlift and sealift capability, and the capacity for rapid response, manoeuvrability and mobility.

Given the implications of state fragility for conflict in Africa, the demand for peace operations on the continent is likely to grow. South Africa's reputation as perhaps the most militarily capable African state means that these problems are likely to become its problems. As a consequence, South Africa will be expected to play a pivotal role in the African Capacity for Immediate Response to Crises (ACIRC) force and in AU-mandated coalitions before the establishment of the ASF. However, as the *South African Defence Review 2014* mapped out in exhaustive detail, the SANDF is in no position to play such a role without a substantial increase in resources; a funding crisis has rendered it incapable of fulfilling its current responsibilities. Yet, in view of more compelling claims on the public purse, there is little prospect of a sizeable increase in the defence budget.

An ailing giant

The SANDF's current crisis in capability and operational effectiveness has been a long time in the making. In 1994 defence spending stood at less than 3% of GDP and around 10% of government expenditure, compared to approximately 4.4% of GDP during the apartheid era.[11] By 2004, the defence budget stood at around 1.5% of GDP; by 2015, it had fallen to around 1.1% of GDP.[12] It is unlikely to rise much above 1% in the foreseeable future. These are not levels of spending consistent with hegemonic power. Arguing that South Africa has underfunded its military for at least a decade, Jakkie Cilliers claims that developing countries without pretensions to regional leadership normally spend around 2% of GDP on

Figure 1: **South African defence spending and GDP per capita**

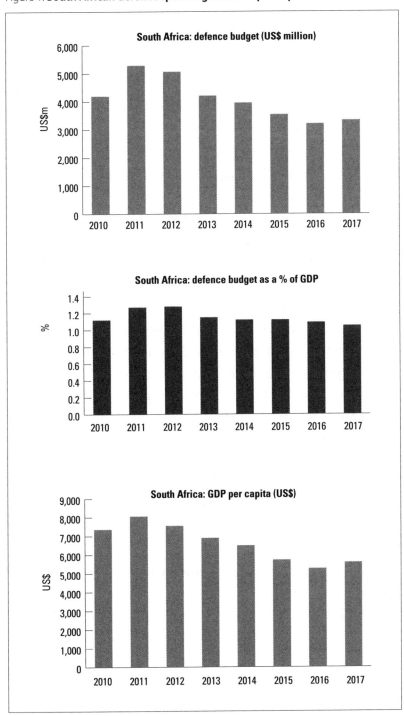

Source: Military Balance+

defence.[13] In 2016 Angola and Algeria spent around US$3billion and US$10.2bn on defence respectively – yet neither country has regional ambitions comparable to those of South Africa, which spent around US$3.2bn.[14]

Alex Vines notes that, as far back as 2004, two UN inspections found much of the SANDF's equipment deployed to the DRC, including 13 of 18 armoured personnel carriers, to be non-operational, meaning that the force was unable to fulfil its mandate. He also bemoaned a lack of funding to 'carry out proper training and ensure the availability of the appropriate equipment to carry out the roles the SANDF has been tasked to perform'.[15] He criticised the standard of training, discipline and equipment of the South African forces participating in the UN Organization Stabilization Mission in the Democratic Republic of the Congo (MONUSCO). In all areas, he reported, South Africa's standards were no higher than those of other African states participating in the mission. Finally, Vines criticised politicians' failure to appreciate the weaknesses of the SANDF and the limitations imposed upon it by the financial framework within which it was being forced to operate.[16] In 2009 then-defence minister Sisulu suggested that a decaying military infrastructure and the loss of skilled personnel were likely to seriously inhibit South Africa's capacity to deploy peacekeeping forces in Africa.[17] In 2010 Hussein Solomon identified several chronic weaknesses in the SANDF that were hindering its ability to provide leadership in the SADC Brigade and undermining its deployments in a variety of peace-support missions. He painted a picture of a force that was 'shoddy and ill-disciplined'[18] and unready for combat due to the age of its troops, their lack of physical fitness (with half of its 76,000 troops unfit for duty) and the 'deplorable state' of its equipment. Solomon asked how South Africa could be 'a regional powerhouse' and a 'strong actor for peace and security' when its armed forces appeared to be neither professional nor effective.[19] In 2012 Pretoria's draft defence review painted an equally bleak picture of operational readiness in the SANDF.[20] The following year, Lucy Dunderdale lamented the SANDF's shortage of resources, lack of training for peacekeeping, high HIV/AIDS infection rates and serious skills shortages. Added to these problems was the high incidence of ill-discipline, misconduct and abuse allegations made against SANDF soldiers serving in peace missions in the DRC and Burundi.[21] In March 2014, a few weeks before the publication of the defence review, the Parliamentary Portfolio Committee on Defence reported that 62% of SANDF facilities, including half of the force's living quarters, were in an unacceptable condition.[22]

Against this backdrop, the *South African Defence Review 2014* came as the first major assessment of the SANDF's operational capacity since 1998, aiming to set the broad trajectory of defence policy over the next two decades and to articulate the principles underpinning it. Largely amplifying the concerns discussed above, the review provided the most penetrating, detailed account to date of the steady demise in the armed forces' operational effectiveness. It highlighted a 'critical state of decline' in the condition of the SANDF,[23] which had become 'too poorly equipped and funded to execute the widening spectrum of tasks to the desired level'.[24] The review directly challenged the complacent assumption that the SANDF was 'militarily the most powerful, effective, best resourced and capacitated country on the African continent'[25] by noting that the army was 'no longer in a position to conduct major combat operations'. Adding that the air force remained 'critically underfunded', the review found that all of these factors were having 'a direct impact upon [the SANDF's] ability to maintain combat readiness across the full spectrum of operational tasks expected of it'.[26] It lamented the erosion of South Africa's military prowess caused by the contraction of the defence budget. Echoing Dunderdale, the review catalogued a range of deficiencies that were undermining the SANDF's capacity to act and, in turn, South Africa's image. These included depleted ammunition stocks; poor, often obsolete, equipment and infrastructure; a preponderance of unskilled and/or ageing personnel; high incidence of HIV/AIDS among soldiers; a lack of a well-trained, capable reserve force; inadequate coordination between military branches; a shortage of modern transport aircraft to support the deployment of forces for peace operations; a lack of infantry trucks; and a skewed balance of expenditure, in which personnel, capital equipment and operational expenses accounted for 52%, 8% and 40% of costs respectively (the review recommended a balance of 40%, 30% and 30%).[27]

The review was candid about the mismatch between South Africa's regional ambitions and the underfunding of its armed forces:

> The persistent disconnect between the defence mandate, South Africa's growing defence commitments and the resource allocation has eroded defence capabilities to the point where the Defence Force is unable to fully fulfil its constitutional responsibility to defend and protect South Africa and its people, and is hard pressed even to maintain its current modest level of commitments.[28]

It added that:

> Even with an immediate intervention, it could take at least five years to arrest the decline and another five years to develop a limited and sustainable defence

capability. The longer the neglect is perpetuated, the greater the effort, time and cost that would be necessary to arrest the decline and restore the minimum capabilities required to safeguard South Africa's borders, protect its maritime trade routes, conduct peace missions and humanitarian interventions, safeguard South Africa and its people and defend and protect the country against external aggression.[29]

The practical consequences of this deterioration are such that South Africa increasingly lacks the capacity for effective intervention in other African states, both unilaterally and as part of a multilateral mission. Its forces in the field are overstretched and suffer from a lack of logistical support, transport aircraft and close air support, as well as more basic materiel such as infantry trucks, ammunition and night-vision equipment. Indeed, the review confirmed the suspicions generated by South Africa's calamitous March 2013 experience in the CAR, where its forces had originally been deployed to train and build the capacity of that country's armed forces. However, when a rebellion against president François Bozizé broke out, the mission appeared to evolve into an attempted defence of his authoritarian regime. South Africa deployed an extra 200 troops to protect its equipment and trainers, only to see 13 of its soldiers killed and 27 others wounded. The casualties came in a battle at Bangui in which 3,000 rebels attacked 280 lightly armed South African troops, while the SANDF's senior generals failed to find sufficient transport aircraft to provide reinforcements.[30] Chastened, the SANDF withdrew from the CAR shortly thereafter in an exercise that reflected the broader malaise in the force. The mission served as an object lesson in how not to engage in an intervention: South African troops had been deployed on the basis of a vague and ambiguous mandate, with weak regional support, no clear exit strategy and insufficient firepower. After the CAR declined into anarchy following the South African withdrawal, France intervened to stabilise the country. Yet by taking a leading role in military intervention and conflict management in Africa, the former colonial power dealt a blow to African agency and demonstrated the limited application of the idea of 'African solutions to African problems'. (This effect could also be seen in France's interventions in Côte d'Ivoire in 2011 and Mali in 2014, and in NATO states' intervention in Libya in 2011.)

Unlike the debacle in the CAR, South Africa's mission in the eastern DRC in 2013 showed what its forces could achieve if properly resourced and equipped. Pretoria deployed 1,300 troops to the DRC as part of the UN Force Intervention Brigade (itself part of MONUSCO), within which South African *Rooivalk* helicopter gunships played a key part in shifting the military balance against M-23 rebels.[31] The CAR and the DRC experiences offer two contrasting visions of how the South African military's future in Africa could take shape, depending on the nature of the government's response to the 2014 defence review. The review states clearly that the government must fundamentally revamp the SANDF if the force is to fulfil its mandate, concluding:

> South Africa's military capability must therefore be commensurate with South Africa's international status, strategic posture and inescapable continental leadership role. The Defence Force must make a vital and unique contribution that complements South Africa's diplomatic efforts, enhances South Africa's influence within wider international developments, and promotes regional security, specifically through the application of military capabilities to pressing African security issues.[32]

The review recognises that it is untenable for South Africa to assume ever greater continental responsibilities, or even sustain its existing responsibilities, out of a sense of African duty without the financial or military means to conduct credible operations. To do otherwise would create an illusion of action while setting South African intervention forces up for failure and endangering the lives of soldiers. Roelf Meyer, chairman of the Defence Review Committee, placed a stark choice before the government when summarising the report:

> There must either be a greater budget allocation or a significantly scaled down level of ambition and commitment which is aligned to the current budget allocation. In short, there are two strategic options available for government: budget must be determined by policy or budget must drive policy.[33]

Response to the 2014 defence review

The review estimated that, in view of South Africa's regional commitments, the SANDF was 24% underfunded.[34] Given this shortfall, the review favoured a radical intervention to arrest the SANDF's decline in the short and medium terms, as well as greater long-term investment to create a sustainable military able to deliver on its core functions of border defence and participation in multinational peacekeeping, as well as peace-enforcement missions on the continent. Although non-military conflict-resolution processes remain a crucial area of South African expertise, some African conflicts – particularly those involving actors who are uncommitted or actively hostile to such processes – may require the deployment of military power.[35] To restore defence spending to an adequate level, the review recommended an increase of R11.7bn (US$813million), or 20.5%, in 2014–15, and of R11.2bn (US$779m), or 18.9%, in 2015–16.[36] Subsequent annual increases would average 6.8% between 2017 and 2028 (as the average increase in 2009–14 was 6.4%, this was not viewed as dramatic).[37] Defence specialist Helmoed-Römer Heitman identifies three distinct phases in the effort to rebuild the SANDF's capacity: halting the current decline, meeting current needs and then meeting future needs. He calculates that rebuilding the force's capability to 189,000 personnel and 158 combat units would require an increase in the defence budget to 1.4% of GDP in the short term, 1.6% of GDP in the medium term and 2.4% of GDP from 2023 – a total increase of R88bn (US$6.1bn).[38] Heitman sees these rises as essential if the government is to give the SANDF the 'minimum capabilities for its projected role and responsibili- ties' in Africa.[39] As well as enabling the SANDF to conduct its designated functions more effectively, this funding would help the force reorient its doctrine, posture and skill set towards the new security environment,[40] and to adapt to emerging threats. Without such a reorientation, even a well-resourced SANDF might prove to be unprepared for the types of conflicts and enemies it is likely to confront.

The review recognised that a core function of any government is prioritisation, effectively pressuring the Zuma administration to determine the purpose of its foreign policy and to define its continental posture. Put simply, South Africa's continental ambitions were radically out of step with the resources allocated to pursuing them. To paraphrase a comment frequently heard during the UN peacekeeping calamities of the 1990s: if South Africa wills the ends, then it must also will the means. However, even if a defence budget is, as Meyer argues, 'a clear indication of how seriously a country takes its national security',[41] there is little evidence that the review caused a change of policy or is likely to do so in the time frame above. Thus,

Cilliers' claim that the review is 'an important first step in the rejuvenation of the SANDF'[42] seems to be based more on hope than expectation. Nosiviwe Mapisa-Nqakula, South Africa's defence minister, formally accepted both the conclusions and recommendations of the report, saying that the government had no choice but 'to respond with urgency' to its findings.[43] However, since the report's publication, the government has demonstrated no urgency in addressing the weaknesses of the SANDF. This attitude was evident in the delay in establishing a parliamentary joint standing committee to consider the report, finally agreed on in October 2014. Moreover, Heitman's claim in September 2014 that 'we have about two years to arrest the decline before it becomes permanent'[44] suggests that the window of opportunity has already closed. As shown in Figure 1, defence spending since the review's publication falls far short of recommendations.

Barriers to increasing the defence budget

To implement the recommendations of the defence review, the government would have to overcome two significant barriers. The first is the factional nature of the ANC, which has produced a political system that centres on the need to balance the interests of various internal groups, virtually paralysing decision-making. Zuma's desire to accommodate these factions – some of them fiercely opposed to significant levels of defence expenditure; others more favourably disposed to a strong South African military presence in Africa – has complicated his attempts to respond to the review coherently. As on so many other issues, complex ANC interests led to an approach that was designed to please all factions but actually pleased none of them. In practice, this amounted to a formal commitment to enhance SANDF capabilities but no significant commitment to allocate additional resources in line with the review. Due to the divided nature of the ANC, and Zuma's lack of ideological conviction and policy substance, the government has allowed drift, deferral and equivocation to effectively become its operating principles.

The second obstacle is even more formidable. The recommendations of the review are disconnected from contemporary political realities in South Africa. Given the scale of South Africa's domestic challenges (see Chapter Three) and the fact that – like most African states – the country's principal security challenges are internal, the renewal of the SANDF is a relatively low priority for the government. As Abel Esterhuyse put it, 'there is no fat in the national budget for defence'.[45] Beyond the military establishment, there is no strong constituency that supports an increase in defence expenditure, as most South Africans understand that this would come at the expense of domestic needs.[46] Even if the ANC was at the height of its electoral popularity, it would be difficult to imagine a situation in which the government could retain its support base while calling for a significantly higher level of defence spending. Indeed, the fact that the SANDF is in the beleaguered condition highlighted by the review reflects a steady downgrade of the force in favour of domestic priorities. With the ANC facing low economic growth and an unprecedented threat to its electoral dominance, it is almost certain to maintain this approach. Already accounting for 60% of government expenditure,[47] social spending may rise further in view of the resulting political pressure, leaving little scope for defence.

The ANC's efforts to protect and rebuild its support base over the next few years will require a single-minded focus on domestic change. Although it is unclear whether such change will occur – the ANC's overall post-1994 record is uneven, while Zuma's is extremely poor – the attempt will not involve a significant reallocation of resources to the military. Greg Mills captured this mood quite accurately:

> Those, for example, scraping by in the eastern Cape on a combination of child support grants, remittances or state pensions and the protein of bones, at R5 a bag, will take some convincing of the benefits to them of fighters and corvettes at R350 million and R2.5 billion respectively.[48]

Although a stable Africa is certainly in the South African national interest, for Pretoria the benefits of this stability are likely to be intangible and slow to take effect, whereas the price of achieving it – through increased defence expenditure – will be borne in the here and now. The debacle in the CAR – and the unclear motivations behind South Africa's mission there – may have curbed Pretoria's appetite for intervention rather than, as argued by Peter Fabricius, serving as a catalyst for a more wide-ranging and assertive role in Africa.[49] Furthermore, an expansive South African military role in Africa does not appear to have commercial or other material benefits. As the 2012 National Development Plan pointed out, South Africa 'has gained little by way of expanded trade and investment opportunities' in African countries where it has been militarily engaged.[50] The ANC knows that the fundamental overhaul of the SANDF recommended by the 2014 defence review will be a gift to its parliamentary opponents. The populist Economic Freedom Fighters routinely seeks to outflank the ANC on the left and to portray itself as the authentic voice of the poor. As part of this, the party has made clear that the money would be better spent on social provision than on the military.[51] Similarly, the Democratic Alliance, a party making electoral inroads in black communities, views the proposed large-scale refurbishment as unaffordable and a 'non-starter'.[52] Given the hostility to its aims among supporters of the ANC and newly empowered opposition groups, the defence review is likely to be of limited practical significance. It is in the context of these persistent political realities that observers should view idealistic conceptions of South Africa's continental role, such as Foreign Minister Maite Nkoana-Mashabane's bombastic 2013 declaration that, when called upon to intervene in 'situations of strife', South Africa 'will always be there, we will never say no'.[53]

Without an increased financial commitment, South Africa will struggle to maintain its military operation in the DRC, which involves 1,350 troops, and its anti-piracy operation in the Mozambique Channel, which involves 220 personnel.[54] It will also be unable to take up a significant role in the ACIRC, despite the fact that Zuma has committed South Africa to being among the countries to contribute to the rapid-deployment force. As Heitman observes, 'the biggest problem here is that the military simply doesn't have enough warm bodies to both patrol our borders and participate in the large-scale deployments it is committed to on the continent'.[55] Andre Roux has noted that while these may seem relatively modest commitments for a force with 40,000 troops at its disposal, one must factor in the high incidence of HIV/AIDS in the armed forces and the fact that, for every soldier in the field, the SANDF also requires another to be preparing for deployment and yet another to be recovering from deployment. As a consequence, he argues, 'when you put these parameters down suddenly you find you don't have the troops you thought you did'.[56] Since 2009, the SANDF has committed 2,500 troops on border-patrol duty – after relieving a police force that had failed to properly fulfil this task – and, in a disturbing echo of the past, has been deployed internally to help quell xenophobic attacks (see

Chapter Two).[57] All of this means that the SANDF is stretched extremely thinly and therefore unable to satisfactorily perform its three core tasks: border defence, internal deployment and African peace operations. Indeed, in July 2017, more than three years on from the publication of the review, Sam Gulube, the secretary of defence, warned South Africans in the starkest possible terms that 'the resources available to the SANDF are no longer adequate to ensure that the territorial integrity of our country is adequately secured'.[58]

The defence department also continues to suffer from the treasury's control of UN funding designed to compensate South Africa for its peacekeeping contributions, which is not always diverted back into the SANDF.[59] Having boxed itself into a corner with rhetoric about the extensive peacekeeping role South Africa can play on the continent, the government would take a considerable risk by continuing to pursue the role without satisfactorily addressing the issues raised in the review. This could lead to more CAR-style military disasters, an even greater humiliation than would come from an honest recognition of South Africa's limitations. In this, Adam Quinn's observations on overreach in American foreign policy also apply to South Africa:

> A responsible leadership must formulate its policy on the basis of some estimation of the nation's existing relative power resources and their expected future level. If there is a significant mismatch between the capacities assumed by a government's policies and the contextual reality, one can expect the policies in question to end badly.[60]

Although South African defence spending is among the highest in Africa,[61] this does not necessarily mean it is equipped for continental leadership. The 2014 review made a strong case for devoting a greater share of resources to the SANDF but, ultimately, this course of action is almost impossible in the country's existing political and economic climate. Nonetheless, this does not mean that the government is forced to, as Heitman suggests, either fund the SANDF to the level recommended by the review or 'completely withdraw from the continent and lose our say in what happens there'.[62] There is a spectrum of options available in which South Africa can still play an important role in African conflict management. This can be best achieved through a prioritisation of the SADC zone, which has become a sufficiently large and complex area since 1997, when it grew to include the DRC. By confining its peacekeeping activities to the sub-region, South Africa can focus on countries in which its interests are most obviously at stake and whose political dynamics it understands relatively well.[63] Although success within the SADC zone is hardly guaranteed and South Africa often stokes anxieties about its potential dominance there, this approach is more feasible than engagement with wider Africa, in which Pretoria's ambitions are likely to outstrip its capacity to make a difference. The transition to a more modest and pragmatic role would be difficult for South Africa, as it would challenge the country's self-image as a great and indispensable African, rather than merely *Southern* African, power. But this is a far better outcome than allowing geopolitical vanity or domestic political drift to push the country down a road that is financially and militarily unsustainable, and that would endanger the lives of South African soldiers. Guy Martin summed up the reality Pretoria faces when he noted that 'one does not do more with less; one does less with less'.[64] In view of this fact, however one chooses to define South Africa's new role, it is unlikely to be that of a hegemon.

South Africa in Africa: The challenges of the new multipolarity

South Africa's capability, both material and ideational, to assume the role of a hegemonic power in Africa in the democratic era was deficient during the presidencies of Nelson Mandela, Thabo Mbeki and Jacob Zuma. In the Mandela era (1994–99) South Africa adopted a diffident, generally low-key role in terms of force projection in the region and sub-region (the atypical 1998 Lesotho intervention notwithstanding), perhaps unsurprisingly in the aftermath of an era of apartheid aggression in Southern Africa. An attempt was made, however, to promote its values of democracy, human rights and conflict resolution as wider African values, behaviour more typical of a hegemon. This effort foundered with failures in Angola (1994), Nigeria (1995) and Zaire/DRC (1997/8), after which Pretoria's championing of those values became more hesitant, tentative and sporadic. The main successes of South African diplomacy in the Mandela period came via its adoption of an energetic middle-power role in building bridges between North and South, for example with the South African-sponsored compromise at the Non-Proliferation Treaty (NPT) review conference in 1995 which allowed that treaty to be indefinitely extended, and in brokering the 1999 deal to end the Lockerbie crisis between the US and the UK on one hand and Gadhafi's Libya on the other. Pretoria was carving out a role for itself in the international arena as a problem-solver, mediator and all-round good international citizen.

Under Mbeki (1999–2008), there was a gradual but identifiable move away from this middle-power posture. His initial commitment to the idea of an African Renaissance and subsequently to the New Partnership for Africa's Development (NEPAD) project as central planks of his foreign policy – each of which stressed the need for clean, accountable and democratic government – had suggested Mbeki was interested in continuing with both a human-rights-oriented policy and a bridge-building role. Eventually, however, Mbeki's foreign policy moved in a more ideologically strident direction in which foreign policy was defined by its strong pan-Africanist character. This found expression in a focus on the need to democratise the institutions of global governance and to build African (regime) solidarity and the continent's multilateral structures. These positions were often laced with a pronounced hostility to Western interference and supposed double standards. This hostility informed Mbeki's approach to conflicts in Darfur (Sudan), and more prominently in Zimbabwe, as South Africa sought to define itself as an emerging power of the Global South rather than as a mediator and bridge-builder. The Zuma presidency since 2009 has failed to make a distinctive impression in the foreign-policy field. True, the invitation to join BRICS in 2010 was extended during his tenure but most of the foundations for South African membership had already been laid in the Mbeki era. Despite initially adopting a more emollient tone in his relations with the West, foreign policy showed great continuity with the Mbeki era. There has been a strong emphasis on building the BRICS relationships at the expense of the West coupled with strong opposition to the West on Zimbabwe, Libya (eventually), Syria and the ICC's indictment of President Omar al-Bashir of Sudan. However, this book contends that South Africa's BRICS membership is potentially problematic for its relations with Africa. BRICS, Russia apart, embraces some of the biggest players in the Global South and it is likely that, as they collaborate on global issues and forge common positions, it will become increasingly difficult for this new oligarchy of the Global South to act as authentic representatives of the smaller Southern states in global multilateral forums. The contention that what is good for Brazil, China, India and South Africa is inevitably good for Sri Lanka, Vietnam, Bolivia and Benin is likely to become unsustainable. The more powerful these larger states become, the more disconnected they will be from those whose interests they purport to champion and the more resentment they are likely to foster. This highlights one of the paradoxes of South African regional policy in the democratic era: namely, support for the country to assume the role of Africa's indispensable leader is considerably stronger from outside the continent than from within it. Overall, South Africa has been a reluctant hegemon throughout this period due to its determination to compensate, and perhaps overcompensate, for an overbearing past, the strong resentment and opposition which it generates in Africa, and a recognition that its power wanes the further it moves beyond its 'near abroad' in the SADC zone. The preceding chapters have sought to map out in detail the difficulties which South Africa confronts as it seeks to assert influence in Africa and, in the view of the writer, these present insurmountable obstacles to a hegemonic role.

South Africa's image or reputational problems on the continent are fuelled by the perception that it remains insensitive to African opinion and is too inclined to view its own interests as synonymous with the wider African interest.

Particularly damaging to Pretoria's standing has been the spate of xenophobic attacks on other Africans in the townships and informal settlements of South Africa and the perception that it preaches the language of economic justice while pursuing its own narrow economic self-interest, often to the detriment of African states, a perception reinforced by the expansion and behaviour of South Africa's corporate sector in Africa. Nor can it be complacently assumed that South Africa's democratic ideals and approach to conflict resolution enjoy widespread support on the continent; all too frequently they attract indignation, bemusement and outright opposition. That said, South Africa's important contributions to the wellbeing of the continent have often been underplayed and even eclipsed by these grievances. South Africa has been an important provider of public goods through its role in peace operations, the design of a continent-wide security architecture, the provision of generous levels of development assistance and in its attempts to at least articulate the African case in global multilateral forums. Moreover, while South African companies are viewed as predatory and expansionist actors – accused of undermining local entrepreneurial activity – these perceptions are rather one-dimensional in that they ignore the significant role those companies have played in reviving transport and communications infrastructure, stimulating dormant African economies and generating employment. Too often though, South Africa has allowed a damaging and negative narrative to become entrenched regarding its economic involvement on the continent. This points to a failure in its public diplomacy which, in Africa at least, has been overly passive and apologetic.

Domestically, the socio-economic challenges confronting the country – including the failure to address the apartheid era's legacy of income inequality – are on such a scale as to severely restrict the country's ability to help Africa, particularly as the

ANC now finds itself in more straitened political circumstances. This does not mean Pretoria cannot play a constructive role in various ways – mainly through development assistance, trilateral development cooperation and financial transfers within the Southern African Customs Union (SACU), although these are likely to be reduced – but merely that these fall well short of meeting the expectations raised by South African government statements and the more extravagant language of the past, particularly Mbeki's commitment to the African Renaissance.

In the security sphere, the country's armed forces are experiencing a capacity and funding crisis, which was set out in detail by the withering *South African Defence Review 2014*. This report – and, more pressingly, the government's failure to respond to its recommendations – casts a long shadow over the ability of the South African National Defence Force (SANDF) to play an extensive role in African peace operations or even to sustain existing commitments. Indeed, South African officials now question the military's ability to secure the country's own borders, its most basic and minimum function. Whilst any kind of leadership role – still less a hegemonic one – requires a state to have much more in its toolbox than military power, it is also beyond dispute that continental leadership certainly requires a considerable military capacity. This is increasingly problematic given the domestic socio-economic demands on the South African budget and while the case for increased defence expenditure has many persuasive advocates, very few of these are to be found in the ANC itself, whether in its higher echelons or the rank and file.

The cumulative effect of these various pressures has served to undermine South Africa's ability and will to project itself as a natural leader on the African continent; one which sets the regional agenda, establishes its dominant norms and values and inspires a willing followership. Instead this points towards a more complex and potentially more disorderly African environment, with South Africa being compelled to adapt to, and work within, a new multipolarity.

Decline and its consequences

Discussions of decline and its likely consequences have become a staple of US foreign-policy analysis over the post-Cold War period although, ironically, they have often been uncomfortably juxtaposed with commentaries on unipolarity and the unparalleled nature of US power.[1] South Africa now finds itself the subject of a similar debate at the regional level. Consequently, as South Africa's military and economic power wanes and that of competitor states begins to rise – and with its soft power producing only limited results – its political elites must adapt to the demands of a new, more uncertain era in continental geopolitics. Although South Africa will still be a leading African state – and more than 'just another country', in J.E. Spence's famous phrase[2] – it will certainly not be *the* leading state. Even if the political will to do so were there (which it is not), and even if it enjoyed universal African backing (which it does not), South Africa can no longer shoulder the primary responsibility for the delivery of peace, stability and development on the continent. However, that decline, and the recalibration of foreign policy it must inevitably entail, will not be without cost. It will take its toll on South Africa's global reputation, which is closely tied to its leadership role in Africa. That leading role has allowed it to punch above its weight in global forums and was instrumental in securing its admission to BRICS, but if South Africa simply falls back into the African pack then its global influence will be diminished and its diplomatic ambitions – such as membership of a reformed UN Security Council – will suffer a major setback.

South Africa increasingly finds itself in a position where it is difficult, if not impossible, to harmonise the differing demands being placed upon it in terms of its Africa policy. The West expects it to be a champion of democracy and economic reform and its fellow BRICS states expect it to be an unambiguous leader in Africa, but the determined pursuit of each risks alienating African opinion. Should it alienate Africa, then it risks jeopardising any claim to African leadership and that, in turn, threatens its wider international standing. Developing a coherent policy in these circumstances is a complex enterprise, carrying with it the grave danger of miscalculation and the likelihood that virtually any policy option will throw up serious complications – the controversy over its 2015 failure to detain Sudanese President Bashir and comply with the ICC indictment being an obvious case in point. Nor should it be assumed that South Africa's relative decline will automatically be accompanied by a seamless transition to Nigerian pre-eminence. As noted in Chapter Three, Nigeria is something of a 'crippled giant',[3] hampered by insurgencies, unacceptably low standards of governance and the inferior quality of its contributions to UN peace operations.[4] In fact, neither state is currently capable of playing a hegemonic role in Africa and, even if working in tandem, they would struggle to maintain a stable bipolarity. Each state has too limited a reach, too many deficiencies and too congested a domestic agenda. It is also clear that African states will be no happier at the prospect of a Nigeria–South Africa duopoly shaping the continent's future than they were when contemplating the outright hegemony of either.

A concert of African powers?

The 'tangible constraints on the quality and quantity of its diplomatic interventions' and the 'real limitations in terms of material resources'[5] will likely compel South Africa (and

Nigeria) to accept a more modest role in a regional system where no African state enjoys preponderant power and influence. They will be required to work within a new multipolar framework alongside other leading African states to help manage and stabilise the continent. The benign interpretation of this scenario is that it will amount to a managed South African decline that will allay African suspicions of the country and is best viewed as an opportunity rather than a challenge. It satisfies South Africa's need for strategic partners in Africa who are, in Anthoni van Nieuwkerk's view, 'effective, efficient and capable',[6] given that no one state can resolve the myriad political, security and economic issues facing the continent. It heralds an emerging concert of African powers, a cooperative multilateralism in which a range of responsibilities are devolved to the various leading states within their own subregions. Ideally, these would be 'like-minded states' who, in the description of the *South African Defence Review 2014*, are 'committed to the common values of democracy and human rights' and who can act as a 'force for good' on the continent.[7]

The obvious states whom South Africa would view as potential African partners are other regional players such as Nigeria, Ghana, Kenya, Ethiopia, Algeria, Egypt and, in Southern Africa, Angola and Tanzania.[8] However, this scenario throws up a host of imponderables and, while a stable multilateralism is the optimum outcome, the new multipolarity may well take Africa's geopolitics in a quite different direction. Two specific problems loom on South Africa's horizon, complicating any attempt to fashion such a concert of powers.

Firstly, this is clearly a heterogeneous rather than a 'like-minded' group of states, and fashioning a consensus among them – as opposed to a lowest-common-denominator position – may prove a complicated process. There is no obvious unity within such an inter-state grouping and no sense that the positions of this group are likely to be driven by a strong commitment to constitutional government and to democratic values as opposed to the traditional African 'norms' of sovereignty and regime solidarity. In fact, strong authoritarian currents flow through this grouping and, consequently, there will either be open disagreement or, if a consensus is forged, it may be because states such as South Africa are continuing to dilute their own commitments to democracy and human rights as the price for securing unity with a cluster of autocratic regimes and illiberal democracies. South African policy in Sudan and Zimbabwe and its determination to leave the ICC point in this direction. Instead of producing greater order and stability, Africa's new multipolarity may foreshadow a more competitive and conflictual 'age of disorder', to quote Randall Schweller,[9] an era in which discord, instability and fragmentation become normalised, even institutionalised, in African inter-state politics. This 'cacophony of competing voices', in Tony Leon's phrase,[10] may mean that agreement is only possible intermittently, with no state able to act as an overall guarantor of African order. One possible means of bringing greater order to bear on such a situation is through a streamlined process in which continental interests are advanced through cooperation between five leading states, each responsible for a distinct sub-region. However, the idea that Africa can be neatly divided into five zones each regulated by a sub-regional anchor state – Egypt in the north, Nigeria in the west, Ethiopia in the Horn, Kenya in the east and South Africa in southern and central Africa – overlooks the opposition this will certainly generate from other states in those sub-regions. Algeria, Ghana, Eritrea, Sudan, Uganda, Tanzania and Angola, to name only the most obvious, will not be prepared to cede such levels of control and autonomy to a single state which aspires to act as their voice and representative. Far from producing 'African solutions to

African problems', this seems more likely to produce stalemate and a power vacuum which, once again, non-African states may seek to fill through alliances with local powers.

Secondly, and looking beyond the structural weaknesses inherent in any multipolar system, South Africa has problematic relations with some significant African players and these tensions are likely to complicate the building of effective partnerships. Its economic relationship with Kenya has been generally troubled since 1994, even if there has been some modest improvement more recently,[11] and the relationship with Paul Kagame's Rwanda – a state whose African importance outweighs its size – remains acrimonious due to the Rwandan regime's repeated attempts to eliminate dissidents and exiles on South African soil, which caused a significant diplomatic rift in 2014.[12] More crucially, the relationship with Nigeria has been an uneasy blend of cooperation, competition and confrontation since 1994. It reached a high point of cooperation during the Mbeki–Obasanjo era from 1999 to 2008,[13] but became more vexed throughout the Zuma–Jonathan period between 2009 and 2015. This was attributable to tensions arising in several areas: the xenophobic attacks on foreign nationals in South Africa poisoned the atmosphere, as did the behaviour of South African corporations in Nigeria. In addition, the relationship has been peppered with disagreements over the question of African membership of an expanded UN Security Council, policy differences over the Libyan and Côte d'Ivoire crises, and the dispute over the election of the chair of the AU Commission in 2012. In general, however, these tensions flow from a classic struggle for regional pre-eminence between two powerful states of a kind instantly recognisable to realist scholars of international relations. Although a Nigeria–South Africa axis is insufficient to guarantee African stability, both states are nonetheless indispensable if Africa is to act with common purpose to advance its agenda and not find useful initiatives stymied by their mutual hostility.[14] It is to be hoped that the March 2016 Buhari–Zuma summit, which created a more constructive atmosphere, provides the catalyst for a revamping of the relationship and a recognition that confrontation only damages the interests of each state and endangers African progress. A more mature relationship is required in which each state grants the other parity of esteem and South Africa, in particular, seeks to accommodate Nigeria's legitimate desire to 'sit at the high table of global politics'.[15] As of 2017, the relationship had recovered from the outright antagonism of 2015, but both parties and the wider continent need a Nigeria–South Africa relationship that transcends a rather nervous, tentative detente – itself a concept anchored in notions of managed hostility and bounded competition rather than partnership.[16]

Ultimately, fashioning a constructive and pragmatic role for South Africa in these highly complex and fluid global and African environments – one which accommodates (albeit imperfectly) its diverse interests – will require innovation, dexterity and consummate statecraft. Yet, disappointingly, government (and especially ANC) foreign-policy documents have so far failed to map out a clear and coherent vision of South Africa's place in the world. Too often they seem to be dogmatic and ideologically driven, with international relations being viewed in one-dimensional, Manichean terms (West bad, non-Western states or counter-Western blocs good) to the detriment of South Africa's interests. As Landsberg, Qobo and Kornegay have pointed out, ANC attitudes to international relations often appear to be 'frozen in a world that no longer exists'[17] and, reading such documents, it is easy to forget not only that the Cold War itself is over but that South Africa's trade and investment relationship with the European Union and the US comfortably surpasses that with China.

Consequently, there is an urgent need for a more astute and balanced foreign policy; one which nurtures South Africa's myriad contacts, prioritises economic diplomacy over rhetoric and seeks to manage and contain differences where they emerge. As Graham Evans notes, determining a hierarchy of interests is the first task of leadership,[18] but it is one with which South Africa has consistently struggled. Southern Africa will remain South Africa's critical security and political relationship due to its proximity and because the economies of the sub-region are expected to be the fastest-growing in Africa over the next two decades, something which South African companies are well placed to capitalise on.[19] However, if South Africa continues to offer tacit and sometimes open support for authoritarianism rather than promote democratic and accountable government, it risks storing up future problems and instability for all parties in Angola, DRC, Swaziland, Zambia and Zimbabwe – although a moment of opportunity has now opened up in the latter given the political demise of Robert Mugabe.[20]

Beyond the sub-region, South Africa's interests would be better served by balancing its relationship with both the West and BRICS. Rather than crudely privileging the BRICS relationship at the expense of the West – and thus far BRICS membership has mainly delivered symbolic rather than practical gains – it would be more advantageous if South Africa sought to maximise the benefits and enhance its leverage with each. Geopolitical and geo-economic differences are certain to arise between these power blocs and, as a BRICS member, South Africa will, on occasion, embrace BRICS positions to which the West is strongly opposed. When doing so, however, it needs to minimise the political and economic fallout from these disputes rather than fanning the flames with knee-jerk confrontational language. South Africa (and the wider continent) cannot afford to view the international system in the polarising language of 'camps' and rigid allegiances. Its development needs require a much subtler foreign-policy approach rooted in 'constructive engagement', to use an old phrase. The prospects for that would be greatly enhanced by improving the level of political education within the ANC itself in which its membership developed a greater understanding of the realities, constraints and possibilities of the international system. This would help it to avoid resorting to the kind of militant posturing which often gives ANC foreign-policy discourse the feel of a museum piece and the movement itself the appearance of a beached whale. This also prevents it from adapting to a rapidly changing international environment, the complexity of which does not lend itself to slogans and a superficial radicalism which fails to advance the interests of its own impoverished constituency. Such posturing often manifests itself in expressions of support for highly authoritarian and failed regimes such as those in Syria, North Korea and, until recently, Mugabe's Zimbabwe, which is not the company an outward-looking, constitutionalist and democratic South Africa should be looking to keep.

Africa north of the SADC zone will remain a key area of political and security concern for Pretoria and a policy of detachment is not feasible here. However, it is also the area where South Africa can set itself more realistic targets and scale down its engagements by focusing its contributions (if invited to make any) on specialist niche areas such as advice on mediation, reconciliation, election organisation and constitutional engineering while leaving much of the heavy lifting in security and intervention to others. Economically, South African corporations will remain engaged and eager to pursue new opportunities across the continent, but a more successful engagement will require them to demonstrate much greater sensitivity to local interests. This can best be achieved by introducing a social dimension to their activities which facilitates

skills transfer, endorses labour rights, and develops collabora-
tive projects with national and sub-national administrations
in host states to help accelerate the provision of education,
housing and other amenities, all of which will help to detoxify
the South African brand. Finally, overextension in the Global
South beyond Africa should certainly be avoided, as grand-
standing in that area risks becoming a distraction from the core
interests of, what Graham Evans labelled, 'a small-to middle
sized developing state with strong regional interests existing
on the peripheries of world politics'.[21]

Unfortunately for South Africa, a balanced and nuanced
foreign policy of this kind requires skilful leadership,
intellectual agility and political finesse. Such qualities have
been conspicuous by their absence from the country's politics
throughout the presidency of Jacob Zuma, a wasted decade of
drift, venality and stagnation which has brought South Africa
to a post-1994 nadir. The central question facing South Africa
as it prepares to move into the post-Zuma era is whether the
ANC can self-correct and restore its credibility – battered
over a decade of egregious misrule – as a competent party of
government. While a more able leadership may succeed in
steadying the ship and restoring a degree of confidence, there
now seems to be a deeper malaise at work in South African
politics, one transcending the shortcomings of any individual
leader, however severe, which is the dysfunctional character
and structural weakness of the ANC itself. The ANC may
boast a proud record as a liberation movement, but it has not
been a vehicle for the effective administration of South Africa
since the Mbeki–Zuma feud erupted in 2005, and its sclerotic
condition, corruption and factionalism are impeding orderly
decision-making and impairing the quality of governance
across the entire policy spectrum, domestic and foreign.[22]
These chronic maladies may be moderated under a post-Zuma

leadership – although the continuation of Jacob Zuma's rule by other means is also a possibility[23] – but the ANC's intellectual and ethical decay, now widely acknowledged in the party itself from the deputy-president, Cyril Ramaphosa, and the secretary-general, Gwede Mantashe, down,[24] will be difficult to reverse. This is a movement which no longer sets the national agenda, looks ideologically exhausted and appears to have outlived its political usefulness, its historic mission now accomplished.[25] The key questions now are how rapid its decline will be, the precise form it will take and how the ANC itself will respond to the inexorable dying of the political and electoral light. The answers to these will determine not only the effectiveness of domestic policy and the trajectory of the country's foreign relations – both in Africa and beyond – but, more fundamentally, they will determine the viability and future of South African democracy itself.

NOTES

Introduction

1 Garth le Pere, 'Critical Themes in South Africa's Foreign Policy: An Overview', *Strategic Review for Southern Africa*, vol. 36, no. 2, 2014, p. 50.

2 Richard Haas, 'The Age of Non-polarity: What Will Follow US dominance?', *Foreign Affairs*, vol. 87, no. 3, 2008.

3 Adam Habib, 'South Africa's Foreign Policy: Hegemonic Aspirations, Neoliberal Orientations and Global Transformation', *South African Journal of International Affairs*, vol. 16, no. 2, 2009, p. 150.

4 Greg Mills and Simon Baynham, 'South African Foreign Policy, 1945–1990', in Greg Mills (ed.), *From Pariah To Participant: South Africa's Evolving Foreign Relations, 1990–1994* (Johannesburg: South African Institute of International Affairs, 1994), pp. 16–18.

5 Stanley Uys, 'The Short and Unhappy Life of CONSAS', *South Africa International*, vol. 18, no. 4, 1988.

6 Kenneth Grundy, *The Militarization of South African Politics* (London: I.B. Tauris, 1986).

7 Joseph Hanlon, *Beggar Your Neighbours: Apartheid Power in Southern Africa* (London: Catholic Institute for International Relations and James Currey, 1986); Robert Jaster, *The Defence of White Power: South African Foreign Policy Under Pressure* (Basingstoke: Macmillan, 1988).

8 Olusola Ogunnubi, 'Recalibrating Africa's Geo-Political Calculus: A Critique of South Africa's Hegemonic Status', *Politikon*, vol. 42, no. 3, 2015, p. 403.

9 Chris Alden and Garth le Pere, 'South Africa in Africa: Bound To Lead?', *Politikon*, vol. 36, no. 1, 2009, p. 148.

10 *Ibid.*, p. 150.

11 David Monyae, 'The Evolving Doctrine of Multilateralism in South Africa's Africa Policy', in Chris Landsberg and Jo-Ansie van Wyk (eds), *South African Foreign Policy Review: Volume 1* (Pretoria: Africa Institute of South Africa, 2012), p. 144.

12 Habib, 'South Africa's Foreign Policy', p. 144.

13 Ogunnubi, 'Recalibrating Africa's Geo-Political Calculus', p. 391.

Chapter One

1   Department of International Relations and Cooperation, 'Building a Better World: The Diplomacy of Ubuntu, White Paper on South Africa's Foreign Policy', 13 May 2011, p. 3; Department of International Relations and Cooperation 2006–09 strategic plan, cited in Alex Vines, 'South Africa's Politics of Peace and Security in Africa', *South African Journal of International Affairs*, vol. 17, no. 1, 2010, p. 59.

2   Nelson Mandela, 'South Africa's Future Foreign Policy', *Foreign Affairs*, vol. 72, no. 5, November-December 1993, p. 89.

3   R.L. Swarns, 'South African Business Moves North', *International Herald Tribune*, 19 February 2002.

4   Brennan M. Kraxberger and Paul A. McClaughry, 'South Africa in Africa: A Geo-political Perspective', *Canadian Journal of African Studies*, vol. 47, no. 1, 2013, p. 10.

5   'The Hopeless Continent', *The Economist*, 11 May 2000, http://www.economist.com/node/333429.

6   'The Region's Blundering Elephant', *The Economist*, 14 November 1998, http://www.economist.com/node/175978.

7   Graham Evans, 'The End of the Rainbow', *World Today*, vol. 55, no. 1, January 1999, p. 11.

8   D.E. Murphy, 'South Africa, the New Samaritan', *International Herald Tribune*, 8 March 2000.

9   Jan van Eck, 'Lessons from the Burundi Peace Process', in Kurt Shillinger (ed.), *Africa's Peacemaker? Lessons from South African Conflict Mediation* (Johannesburg: South African Institute of International Affairs, 2009), pp. 167–77.

10 Anthoni van Nieuwkerk, 'A Review of South Africa's Peace Diplomacy Since 1994', in Chris Landsberg and Jo-Ansie van Wyk (eds), *South African Foreign Policy Review: Volume 1* (Pretoria: Africa Institute of South Africa, 2012), p. 93.

11 Gilbert M. Khadiagala, 'South Africa's Role in Conflict Resolution in the Democratic Republic of the Congo (DRC)', in Shillinger (ed.), *Africa's Peacemaker?*, pp. 67–80.

12 Francis Akindes, 'South African Mediation in the Ivorian Crisis', in Shillinger (ed.), *Africa's Peacemaker?*, pp. 140–6.

13 Jakkie Cilliers, 'Life Beyond BRICS? South Africa's Future Foreign Policy Interests', Institute for Security Studies and Frederick S. Pardee Center for International Studies, June 2017, p. 10.

14 Greg Mills, *From Pariah to Participant: South Africa's Evolving Foreign Relations, 1990–1994* (Johannesburg: South African Institute of International Affairs, 1994).

15 J.E. Spence, 'The New South African Foreign Policy: Incentives and Constraints', in F.H. Toase and E.J. Yorke (eds), *The New South Africa: Prospects for Domestic and International Security* (Basingstoke: Macmillan, 1998), p. 157.

16 Adekeye Adebajo, 'South Africa in Africa: Messiah or Mercantilist?', *South African Journal of International Affairs*, vol. 14, no. 1, 2007, p. 29.

17 John Siko, *Inside South Africa's Foreign Policy: Diplomacy in Africa from Smuts to Mbeki* (London: I.B. Tauris, 2014), p. 34; Victor Mallet, 'Democratic S. Africa Finds Its Neighbours Hard to Convince', *Financial Times*, 27 August 1998.

18 Siko, *Inside South Africa's Foreign Policy*, pp. 243–4; 'The Region's Blundering Elephant', *The Economist*; Mallet, 'Democratic S. Africa Finds Its Neighbours Hard to Convince'.

19 Mandela, 'South Africa's Future Foreign Policy ', p. 89.

20 *Ibid.*, p. 97.

21 *Ibid.*, p. 88.

22 Evans, 'The End of the Rainbow', p. 10.

23 Kraxberger and McClaughry, 'South Africa in Africa', p. 117.

24 Siko, *Inside South Africa's Foreign Policy*, pp. 34–5.

25 *Ibid.*, p. 35.

26 Evans, 'The End of the Rainbow', p. 12.

27 *Ibid.*

28 Tshaba Tjemolane, Theo Needling and Albert Schoeman, 'South Africa's Foreign Policy and Africa: Continental Partner or Hegemon?', *Africa Review*, vol. 4, no. 2, 2012, p. 97.

29 'The Region's Blundering Elephant', *The Economist*.

30 Adebajo, 'South Africa in Africa', p. 36.

31 Jim Broderick, *The United States and South Africa in the 1990s* (Johannesburg: South African Institute of International Affairs, 1998).

32 Chris Landsberg, 'South Africa and the Making of the African Union and NEPAD: Mbeki's "Progressive African Agenda"', in Adekeye Adebajo, Adebayo Adedeji and Chris Landsberg (eds), *South Africa in Africa: The Post-Apartheid Era* (Scottsville: University of KwaZulu-Natal Press, 2007), p. 196.

33 Gerrit Olivier, 'Is Thabo Mbeki Africa's Saviour?', *International Affairs*, vol. 79, no. 4, 2003, p. 822.

34 Ian Taylor, 'Africa's Leaders and the Crisis in Zimbabwe', *Contemporary Review*, vol. 280, no. 1,637, 2002, p. 344.

35 Deon Geldenhuys, 'The Challenges of Good Global Citizenship: Ten Tenets of South Africa's Foreign Policy', *Africa Review*, vol. 3, no. 2, 2011, p. 185.

36 Landsberg, 'South Africa and the Making of the African Union and NEPAD', p. 111.

37 Olivier, 'Is Thabo Mbeki Africa's Saviour?', p. 817.

38 Adam Habib, 'South Africa's Foreign Policy', *South African Journal of International Affairs*, vol. 16, no. 2, 2009, p. 143, 146.

39 James Hamill and Donna Lee, 'A Middle Power Paradox? South African Diplomacy in the Post-Apartheid Era', *International Relations*, vol. 15, no. 4, 2001, pp. 43–8.

40 Patrick Bond, *Talk Left, Walk Right: South Africa's Frustrated Global Reforms* (Scottsville: University of KwaZulu-Natal Press, 2004).

41 Garth le Pere, 'Critical Themes in South Africa's Foreign Policy: An Overview', *Strategic Review for Southern Africa*, vol. 36, no. 2, 2014, p. 40.

42 Kofi Annan, 'Two Concepts of Sovereignty', *The Economist*, 16 September 1999, http://www.economist.com/node/324795.

43 Karen Smith, 'R2P and the Protection of Civilians: South Africa's Perspective on Conflict Resolution', South African Institute of International Affairs, March 2015, p. 2.

44 Geldenhuys, 'The Challenges of Good Global Citizenship', p. 182.

45 Gerard Prunier, 'Could the South African Experience of Conflict Resolution Help in Bringing Peace to Darfur?', in Shillinger (ed.), *Africa's Peacemaker?*, p. 106.

46 'The See No Evil Foreign Policy', *The Economist*, 13 November 2008, http://www.economist.com/node/12607346.

47 Michael Gerson, 'The Despots' Democracy', *Washington Post*,

28 May 2008, http://www.
washingtonpost.com/wp-dyn/content/
article/2008/05/27/AR2008052702556.
html.

[48] Olayiwola Abegunrin, *Africa in Global
Politics in the Twenty-First Century*
(New York: Palgrave, 2009), p. 62.

[49] Siko, *Inside South Africa's Foreign Policy*,
p. 41.

[50] Laurie Nathan, 'Interests, Ideas and
Ideology: South Africa's Policy on
Darfur', *African Affairs*, vol. 110, no.
438, 2010, pp. 64–5.

[51] *Ibid.*, p. 57.

[52] *Ibid.*, pp. 56–7, 62, 66–7.

[53] Tjemolane, Needling and Schoeman,
'South Africa's Foreign Policy and
Africa', p. 91.

[54] Nathan, 'Interests, Ideas and Ideology',
p. 62.

[55] Peter Godwin, *The Fear: The Last Days of
Robert Mugabe* (London: Picador, 2010).

[56] Siko, *Inside South Africa's Foreign Policy*,
pp. 41–2.

[57] Abegunrin, *Africa in Global Politics in
the Twenty-First Century*, pp. 73–4.

[58] Simon Allison, 'Analysis: The
Khampepe Report, a Crushing Blow
to SA's Diplomatic Credibility',
Daily Maverick, 17 November 2014,
http://www.dailymaverick.co.za/
article/2014-11-17-analysis-the-
khampepe-report-a-crushing-blow-
to-sas-diplomatic-credibility/#.
V5Sqn7grLIU.

[59] Hussein Solomon, 'South Africa in
Africa: A Case of High Expectations
for Peace', *South African Journal of
International Affairs*, vol. 17, no. 2, pp.
137–8.

[60] Sabelo J. Ndlovu-Gatsheni,
'Reconstructing the Implications of
Liberation Struggle History on SADC
Mediation in Zimbabwe', South
African Institute of International

Affairs, Occasional Paper No. 92,
September 2011.

[61] Le Pere, 'Critical Themes in South
Africa's Foreign Policy', p. 49.

[62] James Hamill, 'South Africa in Africa:
The Dilemmas of Multilateralism',
in Donna Lee, Ian Taylor and Paul
Williams (eds), *The New Multilateralism
in South African Diplomacy* (Basingstoke:
Palgrave Macmillan, 2006), p. 134.

[63] Anthony Butler, 'South Africa's HIV/
AIDS Policy, 1999–2004: How Can It
Be Explained?', *African Affairs*, vol. 104,
no. 417, 2005, pp. 591-614.

[64] Nathan, 'Interests, Ideas and Ideology',
p. 74.

[65] Chris Alden and Maxi Schoeman,
'South Africa's Symbolic Hegemony
in Africa', *International Politics*, vol. 52,
no. 2, 2015, p. 249; Peter Fabricius, 'Are
We Seeing the Emergence of a New
"Zuma Doctrine" on Africa?', Institute
of Security Studies, 2 May 2013, https://
issafrica.org/crimehub/iss-today/are-
we-seeing-the-emergence-of-a-new-
zuma-doctrine-on-africa.

[66] Cilliers, 'Life Beyond BRICS?', p. 7.

[67] *Ibid.*

[68] Chris Landsberg, 'Continuity and
Change in the Foreign Policies of the
Mbeki and Zuma Governments', *Africa
Insight*, vol. 41, no. 4, March 2012, pp.
6–11.

[69] Geldenhuys, 'The Challenges of Good
Global Citizenship', pp. 185–6.

[70] 'See My Name: South Africa's Love
Affair with Russia', *The Economist*, 16
March 2017, https://www.economist.
com/news/middle-east-and-
africa/21718888-old-ties-days-struggle-
are-being-renewed-south-africas-love-
affair.

[71] Mzukisi Qobo and Memory Dube,
'South Africa's Foreign Economic
Strategies in a Changing Global

System', *South African Journal of International Affairs*, vol. 22, no. 2, 2015, pp. 151–2.

72 'Zuma Congratulates Mugabe on Election Win', *Mail & Guardian*, 4 August 2013, https://mg.co.za/article/2013-08-04-zuma-congratulates-mugabe-on-election-win/.

73 Olivier, 'Is Thabo Mbeki Africa's Saviour?', p. 819.

74 'Zuma says he supports 'people of Zimbabwe''', *Independent Online*, 18 November 2017, https://www.iol.co.za/news/special-features/zimbabwe/zuma-says-he-supports-people-of-zimbabwe-12061596.

75 Gerrit Olivier, 'SA plays cheerleader as neighbour Mugabe sets his own house on fire', *Business Day*, 1 November 2017, https://www.businesslive.co.za/bd/opinion/2017-11-01-sa-plays-cheerleader-as-neighbour-mugabe-sets-his-own-house-on-fire/.

76 Alexander Beresford, 'A Responsibility to Protect Africa from the West? South Africa and the NATO Intervention in Libya', *International Politics*, vol. 52, no. 3, 2015, p. 288.

77 Ibid., p. 300.

78 Na'eem Jeenah, 'Engaging with a Region in Turmoil: South Africa and the Middle East and North Africa Region', in Lesley Masters et al., *South African Foreign Policy Review: Volume 2* (Pretoria: Africa Institute of South Africa, 2015), pp. 149–50.

79 Simon Adams, 'Emergent Powers: Brazil, India, South Africa and the Responsibility to Protect', *Huffington Post*, 20 November 2012, http://www.huffingtonpost.com/simon-adams/un-india-brazil-south-africa_b_1896975.html.

80 'South Africa's Foreign Policy: All Over the Place', *The Economist*, 24 March 2011, http://www.economist.com/node/18447027.

81 Olivier and Schoeman, 'Foreign Policy'.

82 Matt Killingsworth, 'ICC Ruling on South Africa and al-Bashir: Pragmatism Wins the Day', *Conversation*, 27 July 2017, https://theconversation.com/icc-ruling-on-south-africa-and-al-bashir-pragmatism-wins-the-day-81500.

83 Ed Cropley, 'In Bashir Fiasco, Pretoria Makes Clear Africa Comes First', Reuters, 15 June 2015, http://www.reuters.com/article/us-safrica-africa-idUSKBN0OV23320150615.

84 'South Africa to Quit International Criminal Court', *Guardian*, 21 October 2016, https://www.theguardian.com/world/2016/oct/21/south-africa-to-quit-international-criminal-court-document-shows.

85 James Macharia, 'South African Court Blocks Government's ICC Withdrawal Bid', Reuters, 22 February 2017, http://www.reuters.com/article/us-safrica-icc-idUSKBN1610RS.

86 Peter Fabricius, 'ANC Government Still Wants an ICC-free Future for South Africa', *Daily Maverick*, 11 June 2017, https://www.dailymaverick.co.za/article/2017-06-11-anc-government-still-want-an-icc-free-future-for-south-africa/.

87 Killingsworth, 'ICC Ruling on South Africa and al-Bashir'.

88 Peter Fabricius, 'South Africa confirms withdrawal from ICC', *Daily Maverick*, 7 December 2017 https://www.dailymaverick.co.za/article/2017-12-07-south-africa-confirms-withdrawal-from-icc/#.Wi-3DEx2trQ.

89 Peter Fabricius, 'South Africa should not withdraw from ICC, needs to project itself as a leader in anti-impunity efforts- NGOs',

Daily Maverick, 8 December 2017, https://www.dailymaverick.co.za/article/2017-12-08-sa-should-not-withdraw-from-icc-needs-to-project-itself-as-a-leader-in-anti-impunity-efforts-ngos/#.Wi-8OEx2trQ; and Max du Plessis, 'South Africa's latest threat to withdraw from the ICC, or, How to Squander Leadership', Daily Maverick, 11 December 2017, https://www.dailymaverick.co.za/article/2017-12-11-south-africas-latest-threat-to-withdraw-from-the-icc-or-how-to-squander-leadership/#.Wi-6Kkx2trQ.

90 Brendan Vickers, 'Towards a New Aid Paradigm: South Africa as African Development Partner', *Cambridge Review of International Affairs*, vol. 25, no. 4, 2012, pp. 547–8.

91 Fabricius, 'Are We Seeing the Emergence of a New "Zuma Doctrine" on Africa?'.

92 Joe Sandler Clarke, 'South Africa's Failure to Arrest Omar al-Bashir is "Betrayal of Mandela's Ideals"', *Guardian*, 24 June 2015, https://www.theguardian.com/global-development-professionals-network/2015/jun/24/south-africas-failure-arrest-al-bashir-not-in-keeping-mandelas-ideals.

93 Department of International Relations and Cooperation, 'Building a Better World', pp. 10–11; African National Congress, 'The ANC in an Unpredictable and Uncertain World that is Characterised by Increased Insecurity and the Rise of Populism', June 2017, pp. 6–8, https://www.scribd.com/document/352276861/ANC-National-Policy-Conference-2017-Discussion-Document-International-Relations.

94 Liesl Louw-Vaudran, 'Is South Africa a Norm Entrepreneur in Africa?', Institute for Security Studies, December 2016,

p. 9, http://dspace.africaportal.org/jspui/bitstream/123456789/36263/1/policybrief94.pdf?1.

95 Sebastien Hervieu, 'South Africa Gains Entry to BRIC Club', *Guardian*, 19 April 2011, https://www.theguardian.com/world/2011/apr/19/south-africa-joins-bric-club.

96 Alan S. Alexandroff, 'South Africa in a Complex Global Order: How and Where to Fit In', *South African Journal of International Affairs*, vol. 22, no. 2, 2015, pp. 254–6.

97 Chris Alden and Maxi Schoeman, 'South Africa in the Company of Giants: The Search for Leadership in a Transforming Global Order', *International Affairs*, vol. 89, no. 1, 2013, p. 115; Cilliers, 'Life Beyond BRICS?', p. 14.

98 Department of International Relations and Cooperation, 'Building a Better World', p. 19.

99 Maxi Schoeman, 'South Africa as an Emerging Power: From Label to Status Consistency', *South African Journal of International Affairs*, vol. 22, no. 4, 2015, p. 431.

100 Adekeye Adebajo, 'ANC Woolly and Chaotic on Foreign Policy', *Business Day*, 26 June 2017, https://www.businesslive.co.za/bd/opinion/columnists/2017-06-26-adekeye-adebajo-anc-woolly-and-chaotic-on-foreign-policy/.

101 Vickers, 'Towards a New Aid Paradigm', p. 548.

102 Chris Alden and Garth Le Pere, 'South Africa in Africa: Bound to Lead', *South African Journal of Political Studies*, vol. 36, no. 1, 2009, p. 150.

103 Jakkie Cilliers, Julia Schünemann and Jonathan D. Moyer, 'Power and Influence in Africa: Algeria, Egypt, Ethiopia, Nigeria and South Africa',

Institute of Security Studies, March 2015, p. 24.

104 Alden and Schoeman, 'South Africa in the Company of Giants', p. 111.

105 Olusola Ogunnubi, 'Recalibrating Africa's Geo-Political Calculus: A Critique of South Africa's Hegemonic Status', *Politikon*, vol. 42, no. 3, 2015, p. 392.

106 Wendell Roelf, 'Neglected South African Military Needs Big Investment', *Business Day*, 26 March 2014, http://www.bdlive.co.za/national/2014/03/26/neglected-south-

african-military-needs-big-investment.

107 Claire Bisseker, 'Wake Up Call for SA as Nigeria's Economy Takes Top Spot', *Business Day*, 7 April 2014, http://www.bdlive.co.za/economy/2014/04/07/wake-up-call-for-sa-as-nigerias-economy-takes-top-spot.

108 Maxi Schoeman, 'South Africa in Africa: Behemoth, Hegemon, Partner or "Just Another Kid on the Block"', in Adebajo, Adedeji and Landsberg (eds), *South Africa in Africa: The Post-Apartheid Era*, p. 94.

Chapter Two

1 Department of International Relations and Cooperation, 'Building a Better World: The Diplomacy of Ubuntu, White Paper on South Africa's Foreign Policy', 13 May 2011, p. 7.

2 Maxi Schoeman, 'South Africa as an Emerging Power: From Label to Status Consistency', *South African Journal of International Affairs*, vol. 22, no. 4, 2015, pp. 432–3.

3 Cited in Suzanne Graham, 'South Africa's Voting Behaviour at the United Nations Security Council: A Case of Boxing Mbeki and Unpacking Zuma?', in Lesley Masters et al. (eds), *South African Foreign Policy Review: Volume 2* (Pretoria: Africa Institute of South Africa, 2015), p. 74.

4 Cited in Deon Geldenhuys, 'The Challenges of Good Global Citizenship: Ten Tenets of South Africa's Foreign Policy', *Africa Review*, vol. 3, no. 2, 2011, p. 183.

5 *Ibid.*, p. 188.

6 *Ibid.*, p. 191.

7 Mzukisi Qobo and Memory Dube,

'South Africa's Foreign Economic Strategies in a Changing Global System', *South African Journal of International Affairs*, vol. 22, no. 2, 2015, p. 154.

8 Maxi Schoeman, Asnake Kefale and Chris Alden, 'It's Time South Africa Tuned into Africa's Views about Its Role on the Continent', *Conversation*, 24 January 2017, https://theconversation.com/its-time-south-africa-tuned-into-africas-views-about-its-role-on-the-continent-71019.

9 Cited in Alexander O'Riordan, 'Is South Africa the World's Most Generous Donor?', South African Civil Society Information Service, 18 March 2015, http://www.sacsis.org.za/site/article/2318.

10 Chris Alden and Garth Le Pere, 'South Africa in Africa: Bound to Lead', *South African Journal of Political Studies*, vol. 36, no. 1, 2009, p. 146.

11 Department of International Relations and Cooperation, 'Building a Better World', p. 26.

12 Brendan Vickers, 'Africa and the Rising Powers: Bargaining for the Marginalized Many', *International Affairs*, vol. 89, no. 3, 2013, pp. 684–5.

13 Peter Fabricius, 'Why No Lift-off for Africa's Branch of the BRICS Bank?', *ISS Today*, 25 May 2017, https://issafrica.org/iss-today/why-no-lift-off-for-africas-branch-of-the-brics-bank.

14 Happy Kayuni and Richard Tambulasi, 'Big Brother or Big Opportunist? South Africa's Enthusiasm for a Multifaceted Relationship with the Rest of Africa', *Africa Review*, vol. 4, no. 1, 2012, p. 31.

15 Centre for Conflict Resolution, *Post-Apartheid South Africa's Foreign Policy after Two Decades* (Cape Town: Centre for Conflict Resolution, 2014), p. 29.

16 Chris Alden and Maxi Schoeman, 'South Africa in the Company of Giants: The Search for Leadership in a Transforming Global Order', *International Affairs*, vol. 89, no. 1, 2013, pp. 123–4.

17 *Ibid*.

18 Alfredo Hengari Tjiurimo, 'Pitfalls and Prospects: Nigeria and South Africa in Africa', allAfrica, 24 March 2015, http://allafrica.com/stories/201503241264.html.

19 David Smith, 'South Africa Faces Backlash Over Xenophobic Attacks on Migrant Workers', *Guardian*, 19 April 2015, https://www.theguardian.com/world/2015/apr/18/south-africa-migrant-workers-protests.

20 Garth le Pere, 'Critical Themes in South Africa's Foreign Policy: An Overview', *Strategic Review for Southern Africa*, vol. 36, no. 2, 2014, p. 48.

21 Susan Booysen, 'Xenophobia: A Conundrum for SA', *Sunday Independent*, 19 April 2015, http://www.iol.co.za/sundayindependent/xenophobia-a-conundrum-

for-sa-1847245.

22 Steven Gordon, 'Xenophobia across the Class Divide: South African Attitude towards Foreigners, 2003–2012', *Journal of Contemporary African Studies*, vol. 33, no. 4, 2015, p. 495.

23 Smith, 'South Africa Faces Backlash Over Xenophobic Attacks on Migrant Workers'.

24 Schoeman, Kefale and Alden, 'It's Time South Africa Tuned into Africa's Views about Its Role on the Continent'.

25 Le Pere, 'Critical Themes in South Africa's Foreign Policy', pp. 48–50.

26 'African Nations Close Ranks after Week of Horror Xenophobic Attacks, Criticism Gets Very Loud', *Mail & Guardian*, 17 April 2015, http://mgafrica.com/article/2015-04-17-african-nations-turn-on-south-africa-after-week-ofhorror-xenophobic-attacks.

27 Jack Spence, 'Realists Wrestle with Radicals', *Mail & Guardian*, 25 August 1995, http://mg.co.za/article/1995-08-25-realists-wrestle-with-radicals.

28 'SA Businesses in Africa Could Feel "Heat" of Xenophobic Attacks', *Mail & Guardian*, 20 April 2015, https://mg.co.za/article/2015-04-20-sa-businesses-could-feel-the-heat-of-xenophobic-attacks.

29 Smith, 'South Africa Faces Backlash Over Xenophobic Attacks on Migrant Workers'.

30 'SA Businesses in Africa Could Feel "Heat" of Xenophobic Attacks'.

31 Sean Jacobs, 'Xenophobia Plagues Rainbow Nation', *Al-Jazeera America*, 20 April 2015, http://america.aljazeera.com/opinions/2015/4/xenophobia-plagues-rainbow-nation.html.

32 Jonisayi Maromo, 'African Nations to Blame for Influx: Zuma', IOL News, 27 April 2015, http://www.iol.co.za/news/

politics/african-nations-to-blame-for-influx-zuma-1850812.

33 Gordon, 'Xenophobia across the Class Divide', p. 504; Jacobs, 'Xenophobia Plagues Rainbow Nation'.

34 Booysen, 'Xenophobia'.

35 Allister Sparks, 'De Klerk Reaches Out to Africa', *Observer*, 26 April 1992.

36 Alden and le Pere, 'South Africa in Africa', p. 154.

37 Southern African Development Community, *SADC Statistics Yearbook 2011*, http://www.sadc.int/information-services/sadc-statistics/sadc-statiyearbook/.

38 South African Development Community, 'SADC Overview, 2003–2012', http://www.resakss.org/region/sadc.

39 Fred Ahwireng-Obeng and Patrick J. McGowan, 'Partner or Hegemon? South Africa in Africa', in Jim Broderick, Gary Burford and Gordon Freer (eds), *South Africa's Foreign Policy: Dilemmas of a New Democracy* (Basingstoke: Palgrave, 2001), p. 58.

40 *Ibid.*, p. 68.

41 Alden and le Pere, 'South Africa in Africa', p. 157.

42 Jakkie Cilliers, 'Life Beyond BRICS? South Africa's Future Foreign Policy Interests', Institute for Security Studies and Frederick S. Pardee Center for International Studies, June 2017, p. 12.

43 Brendan Vickers, 'South Africa's Economic Diplomacy in a Changing Global Order', in Chris Landsberg and Jo-Ansie van Wyk (eds), *South African Foreign Policy Review: Volume 1* (Pretoria: Africa Institute of South Africa, 2012), p. 115.

44 Daniel Workman, 'Top South African Trading Partners', *World's Top Exports*, 15 August 2017, http://www.worldstopexports.com/

top-south-african-import-partners/

45 See report, 'South Africa 2016', The Observatory of Economic Complexity (Massachusetts Institute of Technology Media Lab), available at https://atlas.media.mit.edu/en/profile/country/zaf/.

46 Cilliers, 'Life Beyond BRICS?' pp. 11–12.

47 Qobo and Dube, 'South Africa's Foreign Economic Strategies in a Changing Global System', p. 152.

48 Schoeman, 'South Africa as an Emerging Power', p. 433.

49 Chris Landsberg, 'Sub-continental Entente: Twenty Years of South Africa's SADC Strategy', in Masters et al. (eds), *South African Foreign Policy Review: Volume 2*, p. 124.

50 Luis L. Schenoni, 'The Southern African Unipolarity', *Journal of Contemporary Studies*, August 2017, p. 17.

51 Brendan Vickers, 'Towards a New Aid Paradigm: South Africa as African Development Partner', *Cambridge Review of International Affairs*, vol. 25, no. 4, 2012, p. 545.

52 Ahwireng-Obeng and McGowan, 'Partner or Hegemon?', p. 60.

53 *Ibid.*, p. 66.

54 Alden and Le Pere, 'South Africa in Africa', p. 157.

55 Centre for Conflict Resolution, *Post-Apartheid South Africa's Foreign Policy after Two Decades*, p. 24.

56 Alden and le Pere, 'South Africa in Africa', pp. 160–1.

57 Phillip Nel and Ian Taylor, 'Bugger Thy Neighbour? Ibsa and South–South Solidarity', *Third World Quarterly*, vol. 34, no. 6, 2013, p. 1,101.

58 *Ibid.*, p. 1,102.

59 *Ibid.*

60 *Ibid.*, p. 1,107.

61 Centre for Conflict Resolution, *Post-Apartheid South Africa's Foreign Policy*

after Two Decades, p. 28.

62 Ahwireng-Obeng and McGowan, 'Partner or Hegemon?', pp. 73–4.

63 Chris Alden and Mills Soko, 'South Africa's Economic Relations with Africa: Hegemony and Its Discontents', *Journal of Modern African Studies*, vol. 43, no. 3, 2005, p. 369.

64 Morris Kiruga, 'Conquering Africa', Mail & Guardian, 3 January 2016, http://mgafrica.com/article/2015-12-18-several-false-starts-later-s-african-companies-figure-out-lucrative-kenyan-market.

65 Anna Wroblewska, 'African Expansion Critical for South African Companies', *AFK Insider*, 29 September 2014, http://afkinsider.com/73863/african-expansion-critical-south-african-companies/.

66 Alden and le Pere, 'South Africa in Africa', pp. 156–7, 159–60.

67 Kayuni and Tambulasi, 'Big Brother or Big Opportunist?', p. 27.

68 Judi Hudson, 'South Africa's Economic Expansion into Africa: Neo-colonialism or Development?', in Adekeye Adebajo, Adebayo Adedeji and Chris Landsberg (eds), *South Africa in Africa: The Post-Apartheid Era* (Scottsville: University of KwaZulu-Natal Press, 2007), p. 137.

69 R.L. Swarns, 'South African Business Moves North', *International Herald Tribune*, 19 February 2002.

70 'Nigeria's $5.2 bn Fine against MTN is World's Largest', fin24, 20 November 2015, http://www.fin24.com/Tech/News/nigerias-52bn-fine-against-mtn-is-worlds-largest-20151120.

71 Tshaba Tjemolane, Theo Needling and Albert Schoeman, 'South Africa's Foreign Policy and Africa: Continental Partner or Hegemon?', *Africa Review*, vol. 4, no. 2, 2012, p. 98.

72 Lyal White, 'Emerging Powers in Africa: Is Brazil Any Different?', *South African Journal of International Affairs*, vol. 20, no. 1, 2013, pp. 118, 121.

73 Alden and Soko, 'South Africa's Economic Relations with Africa', p. 385.

74 Vickers, 'South Africa's Economic Diplomacy in a Changing Global Order', p. 131.

75 Anthoni van Nieuwkerk, 'A Review of South Africa's Peace Diplomacy Since 1994', in Chris Landsberg and Jo-Ansie van Wyk (eds), *South African Foreign Policy Review: Volume 1* (Cape Town: Africa Institute of South Africa, 2012), p. 97.

76 Karen Smith, 'Soft Power: The Essence of South Africa's Foreign Policy', in Landsberg and van Wyk (eds), *South African Foreign Policy Review: Volume 1*, p. 79.

77 Alden and le Pere, 'South Africa in Africa', p. 160.

78 Ian Taylor, 'South African "Imperialism" in a Region Lacking Regionalism', *Third World Quarterly*, vol. 32, no. 7, 2011, p. 1,239.

79 Tjemolane, Needling and Schoeman, 'South Africa's Foreign Policy and Africa', p. 99.

80 Babatunde Akinsola, 'Complacency Allowed Nigeria to Steal SA's Lead Way Too Soon', Naija247 News, 17 April 2014, http://naija247news.com/2014/04/complacency-allowed-nigeria-steal-sas-lead-way-soon/.

81 Vickers, 'South Africa's Economic Diplomacy in a Changing Global Order', p. 117.

82 Kayuni and Tambulasi, 'Big Brother or Big Opportunist?', p. 22.

83 Rudolf du Plessis, Winnie Mutung and Aditi Labahadur, '"The Africa We Want": Unpacking the Primacy

of Africa in South Africa's Foreign Policy', *South African Institute of International Affairs*, 4 May 2016, http://www.saiia.org.za/news/the-africa-we-want-unpacking-the-primacy-of-africa-in-south-africas-foreign-policy.

84 George Rautenbach, 'SA's Ignorance of Africa Does Everyone a Disservice', *Business Day*, 15 March 2016, http://www.bdlive.co.za/opinion/2016/03/15/sas-ignorance-of-africa-does-everyone-a-disservice.

85 Vickers, 'South Africa's Economic Diplomacy in a Changing Global Order', pp. 133–4.

86 Vickers, 'Towards a New Aid Paradigm', p. 541.

87 James Hamill, 'South Africa's Deepening Corruption Crisis', *World Politics Review*, 10 January 2012, http://www.worldpoliticsreview.com/articles/11114/south-africas-deepening-corruption-crisis.

88 Stephen Grootes, 'State Capture: Letters Provide the Smoking Gun but is It Enough to Topple Zuma?', *Daily Maverick*, 28 May 2017, https://www.dailymaverick.co.za/article/2017-05-28-state-capture-letters-provide-the-smoking-gun-but-is-it-enough-to-topple-zuma/#.WYRO8IjyvIU; Ranjeni Munasamy, 'ANC NEC's Final Surrender to Zuma–Gupta Capture', *Daily Maverick*, 30 May 2017, https://www.dailymaverick.co.za/article/2017-05-30-anc-necs-final-surrender-to-zuma-gupta-capture/#.WYRVzojyvIW.

89 Public Protector of South Africa, 'State of Capture', 2016, http://www.pprotect.org/library/investigation_report/2016-17/State_Capture_14October2016.pdf; State Capacity Research Project, 'Betrayal of the Promise: How South Africa Is Being Stolen', May 2017,

https://www.businesslive.co.za/rdm/politics/2017-05-26-how-south-africa-is-being-stolen---read-the-shocking-report/; Genevieve Quintal, 'SA on Verge of a Mafia State, Warns South African Council of Churches', *Business Day*, 19 May 2017, https://www.businesslive.co.za/bd/national/2017-05-19-sa-on-verge-of-mafia-state-warns-south-african-council-of-churches/; Organisation Undoing Tax Abuse, 'No Room to Hide: A President Caught in the Act', 28 June 2017, http://us-cdn.creamermedia.co.za/assets/articles/attachments/69697_2.-report.pdf.

90 Justice Malala, *We Have Now Begun Our Descent: How to Stop South Africa Losing its Way* (Jeppestown: Jonathan Ball Publishers, 2015).

91 Rudy Massamba, 'Why Africa's Presidents for Life Are So Afraid to Lose Power', *World Politics Review*, 20 October 2016.

92 Ian Taylor, 'NEPAD Ignores the Fundamental Politics of Africa', *Contemporary Review*, vol. 285, no. 1662, 2004, pp. 31–2.

93 Liesl Louw-Vaudran, 'Is South Africa a Norm Entrepreneur in Africa?', Institute for Security Studies, December 2016, p. 3, http://dspace.africaportal.org/jspui/bitstream/123456789/36263/1/policybrief94.pdf?1.

94 Peter Fabricius, 'No Coup on Our Watch, Says South Africa', *Daily Maverick*, 12 June 2017, https://www.dailymaverick.co.za/article/2017-06-11-lesotho-no-coup-on-our-watch-says-south-africa/.

95 Mmusi Maimane, 'South Africa Must Stand Up for Democracy on the Continent', *Daily Maverick*, 24 April 2017, https://www.dailymaverick.co.za/opinionista/2017-04-20-south-

africa-must-stand-up-for-democracy-on-the-1continent/.

96 Kristina Bentley and Roger Southall, cited in Devon Curtis, 'South Africa: "Exporting Peace" to the Great Lakes Region', in Adebajo, Adedeji and Landsberg (eds), *South Africa in Africa: The Post-Apartheid Era* (Scottsville: University of KwaZulu-Natal Press, 2007), p. 270.

97 Mark Gevisser, 'Strange Bedfellows: Mandela, de Klerk and the New South Africa', *Foreign Affairs*, vol. 79, no. 1, 2000, p. 173.

98 James Hamill, 'A Disguised Surrender? South Africa's Negotiated Settlement and the Politics of Conflict Resolution', *Diplomacy & Statecraft*, vol. 14, no. 3, 2003, pp. 19–26.

99 Kurt Shillinger, 'Learning from South African Engagement in African Crises', in Kurt Shillinger (ed.), *Africa's Peacemaker? Lessons from South African Conflict Mediation* (Johannesburg: South African Institute of International Affairs, 2009), p. 20.

100 Daniela Kroslak, 'South Africa's Implementation of Its Own Peacekeeping Model in Africa: A Reality Check', in Shillinger (ed.), *Africa's Peacemaker?*, p. 42.

101 James Hamill, 'Angola's Road from Under the Rubble', *World Today*, vol. 50, no. 1, 1994, pp. 6–11.

102 Chris Alden and Maxi Schoeman, 'South Africa's Symbolic Hegemony in Africa', *International Politics*, vol. 52, no. 2, 2015, p. 246.

103 John Siko, *Inside South Africa's Foreign Policy: Diplomacy in Africa from Smuts to Mbeki* (London: I.B. Tauris, 2014), p. 34.

104 Tony Leon, 'Where in the World Is South Africa?', *South African Journal of International Affairs*, vol. 20, no. 3, 2013, p. 455.

105 Liesl Louw-Vaudran, 'Is South Africa a Norm Entrepreneur in Africa?', p. 9.

106 Peter Fabricius, 'DRC/SA Talks: Zuma Happy with Technical Delay in DRC Poll', *Daily Maverick*, 26 June 2017, https://www.dailymaverick.co.za/article/2017-06-26-drcsa-talks-zuma-happy-with-technical-delay-in-drc-poll/.

107 *Ibid.*

108 Kwesi Aning, 'Healer or Hegemon? Assessing Perceptions of South Africa's Role and Motivation in African Mediation', in Shillinger (ed.), *Africa's Peacemaker?*, pp. 55–6; Peter Fabricius, 'SA Should First Sort Out Its Own Backyard', *ISS Today*, 20 July 2017, https://issafrica.org/iss-today/sa-should-first-sort-out-its-own-backyard.

109 Mark Tran, 'Zimbabwe Election: Mugabe Threatens to Arrest Opposition Leaders', *Guardian*, 17 June 2008, https://www.theguardian.com/world/2008/jun/17/zimbabwe.

110 René Lemarchand cited in Alexander Beresford, 'A Responsibility to Protect Africa from the West? South Africa and the NATO Intervention in Libya', *International Politics*, vol. 52, no. 3, May 2015, p. 296.

111 James Hamill, 'For Zimbabwe, National Unity Is a Dead End', *Guardian*, 2 July 2008, https://www.theguardian.com/commentisfree/2008/jul/02/zimbabwe.

112 Liesl Louw-Vaudran, 'Is South Africa a Norm Entrepreneur in Africa?', p. 8.

113 Alden and Schoeman, 'South Africa's Symbolic Hegemony in Africa', p. 119.

114 Olusola Ogunnubi, 'Recalibrating Africa's Geo-political Calculus: A Critique of South Africa's Hegemonic Status', *Politikon*, vol. 42, no. 3, 2015, p. 392.

115 Mmanaledi Mataboge and Glynnis

Underhill, 'Humiliated SA Given Its Marching Orders', *Mail & Guardian*, 5 April 2013, http://www.mg.co.za/article/2013-04-05-00-humiliated-sa-given-its-marching-orders.

[116] Cilliers, 'Life Beyond BRICS?', p. 9.

[117] *Ibid.*, p. 7.

[118] *Ibid.*, p. 9.

[119] Savo Heleta, 'Securitising Humanitarian Assistance and Post-conflict Reconstruction in Africa: A Critical Review of South Africa's New Defence Policy', *African Security Review*, vol. 25, no. 1, 2016, p. 7.

[120] Kayuni and Tambulasi, 'Big Brother or Big Opportunist?', p. 23.

[121] Vickers, 'South Africa's Economic Diplomacy in a Changing Global Order', pp. 124–5.

[122] Finmark Trust, 'Factsheet: Remittances from South Africa to SADC', 20 July 2012, http://cenfri.org/documents/Remittances/2012/Remittances%20from%20South%20Africa%20to%20SADC_Fact%20Sheet.pdf.

[123] James Melik, 'Does the Kimberley Process Work?', BBC, 28 June 2010, http://www.bbc.co.uk/news/10307046.

[124] Graham, 'South Africa's Voting Behaviour at the United Nations Security Council', pp. 81, 87, 89.

[125] Victor Mallet, 'Democratic S. Africa Finds Its Neighbours Hard to Convince', *Financial Times*, 27 August 1998.

[126] Smith, 'Soft Power', p. 78.

Chapter Three

[1] Gerrit Olivier, 'SA is Not the Influential Global Player It Thinks It Is', *Business Day*, 12 June 2013, https://www.businesslive.co.za/bd/opinion/2013-06-12-sa-is-not-the-influential-global-player-it-thinks-it-is/.

[2] Norimitsu Onishi, 'ANC Suffers Major Election Setback in South Africa', *New York Times*, 5 August 2016, https://www.nytimes.com/2016/08/06/world/africa/south-africa-election-anc.html.

[3] Chris Alden and Garth le Pere, 'South Africa in Africa: Bound to Lead', *South African Journal of Political Studies*, vol. 36, no. 1, 2009, p. 166.

[4] Nancy L. Clark and William H. Worger, *South Africa: The Rise and Fall of Apartheid* (Harlow: Pearson Education Limited, 2011), p. 171.

[5] Daniel McLaren, 'SA's Promise of True Equality Still a Dream', *Mail & Guardian*, 23 June 2017, https://mg.co.za/article/2017-06-23-00-sas-promise-of-true-equality-still-a-dream/.

[6] Olayiwola Abegunrin, *Africa in Global Politics in the Twenty-First Century: A Pan-African Perspective* (New York: Palgrave, 2009), p. 66.

[7] Chester Crocker, 'South Africa: Strategy for Change', *Foreign Affairs*, vol. 59, no. 2, 1980, p. 323.

[8] McLaren, 'SA's Promise of True Equality Still a Dream'.

[9] Adam Wakefield, 'One in 10 South Africans Living with HIV – Stats SA', *News 24*, 23 July 2015, http://www.news24.com/SouthAfrica/News/One-in-10-South-Africans-living-with-HIV-Stats-SA-20150723.

[10] Garth le Pere, 'Critical Themes in South Africa's Foreign Policy: An Overview', *Strategic Review for Southern Africa*, vol. 36, no. 2, 2014, p. 35.

[11] Abegunrin, *Africa in Global Politics in*

the Twenty-First Century, p. 59.

12 'SA Unemployment Rate Rises to 14-year High', *Daily Maverick*, 1 June 2017, https://www.dailymaverick. co.za/article/2017-06-01-sa-unemployment-rate-rises-to-14-year-high/#.WVthoo2ou7o.

13 Barend Louwrens Prisloo, 'The Security Dilemma Evident in South Africa's Foreign Policy Towards Africa', *Africa Review*, vol. 8, no. 2, 2016, p. 90.

14 Kevin Lings, 'In SA 1 in 4 Still Unemployed – Youth Crisis as 63.1% Remain Jobless', *BizNews*, 29 July 2015, http://www.biznews.com/thought-leaders/2015/07/29/sa-q2-unemployment-eases-to-25-but-63-1-of-youth-remain-jobless/.

15 Greg Nicolson, 'South Africa: Where 12 Million People Live in Extreme Poverty', *Daily Maverick*, 3 February 2015, http://www.dailymaverick.co.za/article/2015-02-03-south-africa-where-12-million-live-in-extreme-poverty/#. V8VbhU2V-7o.

16 McLaren, 'SA's Promise of True Equality Still a Dream'.

17 Maxi Schoeman, 'South Africa as an Emerging Power: From Label to Status Consistency', *South African Journal of International Affairs*, vol. 22, no. 4, 2015, p. 439.

18 Simon Allison, 'Black Economic Empowerment Has Failed: Piketty on South African Inequality', *Guardian*, 6 October 2015, https://www. theguardian.com/world/2015/oct/06/piketty-south-africa-inequality-nelson-mandela-lecture.

19 Alden and le Pere, 'South Africa in Africa', p. 162.

20 Simon Allison, 'Black Economic Empowerment Has Failed'.

21 Schoeman, 'South Africa as an Emerging Power', p. 439.

22 Housing Development Agency, 'Informal Settlements Status (2013)', p. 18, http://www.thehda.co.za/uploads/files/HDA-South-Africa-Report-lr.pdf.

23 'South African Anger at "Worst Maths and Science" Ranking', BBC, 3 June 2014, http://www.bbc.co.uk/news/world-africa-27683189.

24 Wakefield, 'One in 10 South Africans Living with HIV – Stats SA'.

25 McLaren, 'SA's Promise of True Equality Still a Dream'.

26 Stephanie Pretorius, 'SA's Real Level of Literacy', *Citizen*, 29 August 2013, http://citizen.co.za/31407/literatez/.

27 'SA's Business Leaders Generally Downbeat about the Future', *Business Day*, 13 March 2017, https://www. businesslive.co.za/bd/business-and-economy/2017-03-13-sas-business-leaders-generally-downbeat-about-the-future/.

28 'South Africa Economy Data', FocusEconomics, 20 June 2017, http://www.focus-economics.com/countries/south-africa.

29 Ntsakisi Maswanganyi, 'IMF Cuts SA's 2017 Growth Rate Forecast Due to Joblessness and Economic Uncertainty', *Business Day*, 4 October 2016, http://www.bdlive.co.za/economy/2016/10/04/imf-cuts-sas-2017-growth-forecast-due-to-joblessness-and-economic-uncertainty.

30 '0.2 GDP Growth in 2017: South Africa's Dismal Outlook Now that Gordhan Is Gone', *Business Tech*, 2 April 2017, https://businesstech.co.za/news/government/167761/0-2-gdp-growth-in-2017-south-africas-dismal-outlook-now-that-gordhan-is-gone/.

31 Statistics South Africa, 'The South African Economy Shrinks by 0,7%', 6 June 2017, http://www.statssa.gov.

za/?p=9989.

32 James Hamill, 'South Africa's Zuma Faces Double Bind on Troubled Economy', *World Politics Review*, 20 April 2015, http://www.worldpoliticsreview. com/articles/15564/south-africa-s-zuma-faces-double-bind-on-troubled-economy.

33 Lumkile Mondi, 'South Africa Can Expect Zero Growth. Its Problems are Largely Homemade', *Conversation*, 25 July 2016, http://theconversation. com/south-africa-can-expect-zero-growth-its-problems-are-largely-homemade-62943.

34 Hamill, 'South Africa's Zuma Faces Double Bind on Troubled Economy'.

35 'South Africa's Credit Rating Has Been Cut to Junk Status', BBC, 3 April 2017, http://www.bbc.co.uk/news/ business-39476903; Joseph Cotterill, 'Fitch Cuts South Africa's Credit Rating to Junk', *Financial Times*, 7 April 2017, https://www.ft.com/ content/5b8e083c-1b91-11e7-bcac-6d03d067f81f?mhq5j=e1.

36 'Moody's Downgrades SA One Notch, Assigns Negative Outlook', CNBC Africa, 9 June 2017, https:// www.cnbcafrica.com/trending/ sa-downgrade/2017/06/09/ moodys-rates-sa/.

37 Agathe Fonkam, 'Reflections on the Ratings Downgrades', Politicsweb, 23 May 2017, http://www.politicsweb. co.za/opinion/reflections-on-the-ratings-downgrades. Not all downgrades hit borrowing or investment, as seen in the case of the United States.

38 Zinhle Mapumulo, 'Service Delivery Protests Intensifying in Run-up to Elections', *City Press*, 3 June 2016, http://city-press.news24.com/News/ service-delivery-protests-intensifying-in-run-up-to-elections-20160603.

39 Clayson Monyela, 'Letter to the Editor: South Africa Plays an Active Role in the AU', *Daily Maverick*, 11 July 2017, https://www. dailymaverick.co.za/article/2017-07-11-letter-to-the-editor-south-africa-plays-an-active-role-in-the-au/?utm_content=buffercf68c&utm_medium=social&utm_source=twitter. com&utm_campaign=buffer#. WYRaELpFzuh.

40 S'thembiso Msomi, 'The Inside Story of South Africa's Seismic Political Shift', *Rand Daily Mail*, 21 August 2016, http:// www.rdm.co.za/politics/2016/08/21/ the-inside-story-of-south-africa-s-seismic-political-shift.

41 Gerrit Olivier, 'Now Is the Time for SA to Become Exceptional Again', *Business Day*, 22 August 2016, http:// www.bdlive.co.za/opinion/2016/08/22/ now-is-the-time-for-sa-to-become-exceptional-again.

42 Carol Paton, 'After a Polls Thrashing: Quo Vadis, ANC?', *Business Day*, 8 August 2016, http://www. bdlive.co.za/opinion/2016/08/08/ after-a-polls-thrashing-quo-vadis-anc.

43 Department of International Relations and Cooperation, 'Building a Better World: The Diplomacy of Ubuntu, White Paper on South Africa's Foreign Policy', 13 May 2011, p. 18 and pp. 20–3.

44 Alden and le Pere, 'South Africa in Africa', p. 167.

45 *Ibid.*, p. 161.

46 Abegunrin, 'Africa in Global Politics in the Twenty-First Century', p. 68.

47 Mzukisi Qobo and Memory Dube, 'South Africa's Foreign Economic Strategies in a Changing Global System', *South African Journal of International Affairs*, vol. 22, no. 2, 2015,

p. 149.

48 Jakkie Cilliers, Julia Schünemann and Jonathan D. Moyer, 'Power and Influence in Africa: Algeria, Egypt, Ethiopia, Nigeria and South Africa', Institute of Security Studies, March 2015, p. 24.

49 Happy Kayuni and Richard Tambulasi, 'Big Brother or Big Opportunist? South Africa's Enthusiasm for a Multifaceted Relationship with the Rest of Africa', Africa Review, vol. 4, no. 1, 2012, p. 25.

50 John Siko, Inside South Africa's Foreign Policy: Diplomacy in Africa from Smuts to Mbeki (London: I.B. Tauris, 2014), p. 46.

51 Alden and le Pere, 'South Africa in Africa', p. 149.

52 Chris Landsberg, 'Continuity and Change in the Foreign Policies of the Mbeki and Zuma Governments', Africa Insight, vol. 41, no. 4, March 2012, p. 8.

53 Nelson Mandela, 'South Africa's Future Foreign Policy', Foreign Affairs, vol. 72, no 5, 2003, p. 91.

54 Brendan Vickers, 'Towards a New Aid Paradigm: South Africa as African Development Partner', Cambridge Review of International Affairs, vol. 25, no. 4, 2012, p. 547.

55 James Hamill, 'Closing the Door: South Africa's Draconian Immigration Reforms', World Politics Review, 7 October 2014, http://www.worldpoliticsreview.com/articles/14145/closing-the-door-south-africa-s-draconian-immigration-reforms.

56 Kayuni and Tambulase, 'Big Brother or Big Opportunist?', p. 18.

57 South African Department of Defence, South African Defence Review 2014 (Pretoria: South African Department of Defence, 2014), pp. 3, 8.

58 Schoeman, 'South Africa as an Emerging Power', p. 439.

59 Kayuni and Tambulasi, 'Big Brother or Big Opportunist?', p. 30.

60 Alden and le Pere, 'South Africa in Africa', p. 166.

61 Qobo and Dube, 'South Africa's Foreign Economic Strategies in a Changing Global System', p. 156.

62 Brendan Vickers, 'South Africa's Economic Diplomacy in a Changing Global Order', in Chris Landsberg and Jo-Ansie van Wyk (eds), South African Foreign Policy Review: Volume 1 (Pretoria: Africa Institute of South Africa, 2012), p. 116.

63 Chris Alden and Maxi Schoeman, 'South Africa's Symbolic Hegemony in Africa', International Politics, vol. 52, no. 2, 2015, p. 244.

64 Vickers, 'South Africa's Economic Diplomacy in a Changing Global Order', p. 122.

65 Alden and Schoeman, 'South Africa's Symbolic Hegemony in Africa', p. 240.

66 Cilliers, Schünemann and Moyer, 'Power and Influence in Africa', p. 14.

67 Chris Alden and Maxi Schoeman, 'South Africa in the Company of Giants: The Search for Leadership in a Transforming Global Order', International Affairs, vol. 89, no. 1, 2013, pp. 118–19.

68 James Hamill, 'South Africa's Deepening Corruption Crisis', World Politics Review, 10 January 2012, http://www.worldpoliticsreview.com/articles/11114/south-africas-deepening-corruption-crisis.

69 Transparency International, 'Corruption Perceptions Index 2015', http://www.transparency.org/cpi2015#results-table.

70 Tim Cocks, 'Nigeria versus South Africa: size matters but so does development', Reuters, 10 April 2014, https://af.reuters.com/article/topNews/

idAFKBN0CW05G20140410.

71 Azwimpheleli Langalanga, 'SA, Stand Up and Lead Africa!', *Sunday Independent*, 13 April 2014, http://www.iol.co.za/sundayindependent/sa-stand-up-and-lead-africa-1675172.

72 World Bank, 'GDP per Capita (Current US$)', https://data.worldbank.org/indicator/NY.GDP.PCAP.CD; World Bank, 'Population, Total', https://data.worldbank.org/indicator/SP.POP.TOTL.

73 United Nations Development Programme, *Human Development Report 2015* (New York: United Nations Development Programme, 2015), pp. 49–50.

74 Cilliers, Schünemann and Moyer, 'Power and Influence in Africa', p. 10.

75 Olusola Ogunnubi and Ufo Okeke-Uzodike, 'Can Nigeria Be Africa's Hegemon?', *African Security Review*, vol. 25, no. 2, 2016, pp. 116–17.

76 Mo Ibrahim Foundation, 'Ibrahim Index of African Governance', 2015, http://static.moibrahimfoundation.org/u/2015/10/02193252/2015-IIAG-Executive-Summary.pdf.

77 Oxford Business Group, *The Report: South Africa 2016: Capital Markets*, https://www.oxfordbusinessgroup.com/overview/between-two-worlds-jse-seeks-establish-south-africa-global-trading-centre.

78 Alden and Schoeman, 'South Africa's Symbolic Hegemony in Africa', p. 244.

79 'Nigeria Overtakes South Africa as Africa's Biggest Economy', *Guardian*, 19 October 2016, http://guardian.ng/news/nigeria-overtakes-south-africa-as-africas-biggest-economy-imf/.

80 'The Real Lesson of Nigerian GDP', *Business Day*, 8 April 2014, http://www.bdlive.co.za/opinion/editorials/2014/04/08/editorial-the-real-lesson-of-nigerian-gdp.

81 Department of International Relations and Cooperation, 'Building a Better World: The Diplomacy of Ubuntu, White Paper on South Africa's Foreign Policy', p. 20.

82 Savo Heleta, 'Securitising Humanitarian Assistance and Post-conflict Reconstruction in Africa: A Critical Review of South Africa's New Defence Policy', *African Security Review*, vol. 25, no. 1, 2016, p. 12.

83 *Ibid.*, p. 15.

84 Vickers, 'Towards a New Aid Paradigm', pp. 545–6.

85 Heleta, 'Securitising Humanitarian Assistance', pp. 10–12.

86 Department of International Relations and Cooperation, *The African Renaissance and International Cooperation Fund Annual Report for 2015/16 Financial Year*, p. 34, http://www.dirco.gov.za/department/african_renaissence_2015_2016/african_renaissance_fund_2015_16.pdf.

87 Amanda Lucey and Sibongile Gida, 'Enhancing South Africa's Post-conflict Development Role in the African Union', Institute for Security Studies, May 2014, pp. 6–7, https://issafrica.s3.amazonaws.com/site/uploads/Paper256.pdf.

88 Amanda Lucey, 'South Africa's Development Cooperation: Opportunities in the Global Arena', United Nations University Centre for Policy Research, November 2015, p. 3, http://www.saiia.org.za/speeches-presentations-other-events-materials/920-2015-11-24-nest-ssc-event-paper-amanda-lucey-iss/file.

89 Cheryl Hendricks and Amanda Lucey, 'Burundi: Missed Opportunities

for South African Post-conflict Development and Peacebuilding', Institute for Security Studies, October 2013, p. 4, https://www.files.ethz.ch/isn/171280/PolBrief48_9Oct2013.pdf.

90 Le Pere, 'Critical Themes in South Africa's Foreign Policy: An Overview', p. 47.

91 Aditi Lalbahadur, 'South Africa's Economic Statecraft in Southern Africa: Non-existent or Nascent? An Examination of Relations with Zimbabwe and Swaziland', South African Institute of International Affairs, May 2014, p. 7.

92 Peter Fabricius, 'Time to Pull the Plug on SACU?', Politicsweb, 12 March 2015, http://www.politicsweb.co.za/news-and-analysis/time-to-pull-the-plug-on-sacu.

93 Ibid.

94 Alexander O'Riordan, 'Is South Africa the World's Most Generous Donor?', South African Civil Society Information Service, 18 March 2015, http://sacsis.org.za/site/article/2318.

95 Fabricius, 'Time to Pull the Plug on SACU?'.

96 O'Riordan, 'Is South Africa the World's Most Generous Donor?'.

97 Le Pere, 'Critical Themes in South Africa's Foreign Policy', p. 48.

98 Liesl Louw-Vaudran, 'Is South Africa a Norm Entrepreneur in Africa?', Institute for Security Studies, December 2016, p. 10, http://dspace.africaportal.org/jspui/bitstream/123456789/36263/1/policybrief94.pdf?1.

99 Parliamentary Monitoring Group, 'National Council of Provinces Trade and International Relations: South African Development Partnership Agency – Progress Report', 17 February 2016, https://pmg.org.za/committee-meeting/22022/.

100 Vickers, 'Towards a New Aid Paradigm', pp. 551–2.

101 Lesley Masters, 'Building Bridges? South African Foreign Policy and Trilateral Development Cooperation', South African Journal of International Affairs, vol. 21, no. 2, 2014, p. 181.

102 Helen Yanacopulos, 'The Janus Faces of a Middle Power: South Africa's Emergence in International Development', Journal of Southern African Studies, vol. 40, no. 1, 2014, pp. 205, 210–12, 216.

103 Ibid., p. 215.

104 Masters, 'Building Bridges?', pp. 181–2.

105 Ibid., pp. 179, 185, 187.

106 Lucey, 'South Africa's Development Cooperation', p. 5.

107 Jakkie Cilliers, 'Life Beyond BRICS? South Africa's Future Foreign Policy Interests', Institute for Security Studies and Frederick S. Pardee Center for International Studies, June 2017, p. 17.

108 Alden and Schoeman, 'South Africa in the Company of Giants', p. 120.

109 Natasha Marrian, 'ANC stalwarts hoping against hope', Financial Mail, 23 November 2017, https://www.businesslive.co.za/fm/features/2017-11-23-anc-stalwarts-hoping-against-hope/.

110 Graham Evans, 'The End of the Rainbow', World Today, vol. 55, no. 1, January 1999, p. 12.

Chapter Four

1 'Peacekeeping in Africa', *Financial Mail*, 14 February 1997.

2 Anton du Plessis, 'The Military Instrument in South African Foreign Policy: A Preliminary Exploration', *Strategic Review for Southern Africa*, vol. 25, no. 2, 2003, p. 118.

3 Garth le Pere, 'Critical Themes in South Africa's Foreign Policy: An Overview', *Strategic Review for Southern Africa*, vol. 36, no. 2, 2014, p. 46.

4 Anthoni van Nieuwkerk, 'A Review of South Africa's Peace Diplomacy Since 1994', in Chris Landsberg and Jo-Ansie van Wyk (eds), *South African Foreign Policy Review: Volume 1* (Cape Town: Africa Institute of South Africa, 2012), p. 99.

5 Savo Heleta, 'Securitising Humanitarian Assistance and Post-conflict Reconstruction in Africa: A Critical Review of South Africa's New Defence Policy', *African Security Review*, vol. 25, no. 1, 2016, p. 5.

6 Greg Mills, 'An Option of Difficulties? A 21st Century South African Defence Review', Brenthurst Foundation, 2011, p. 19.

7 'The Hopeful Continent: Africa Rising', *The Economist*, 3 December 2011, http://www.economist.com/node/21541015.

8 United Nations Development Programme, *Human Development Report 2015* (New York: United Nations Development Programme, 2015), pp. 49–50.

9 Cited in Heleta, 'Securitising Humanitarian Assistance and Post-conflict Reconstruction in Africa', p. 10.

10 Mills, 'An Option of Difficulties?', p. 20.

11 Ryan Lenora Brown, 'Once a Major Continental Force, South Africa's Military at a Crossroads', *Christian Science Monitor*, 29 June 2015, http://www.csmonitor.com/World/Africa/2015/0629/Once-a-majorcontinental-force-South-Africa-smilitary-at-a-crossroads.

12 'Delay in SANDF Review Costing Armed Forces – Minister', *Citizen*, 19 May 2015, http://citizen.co.za/385566/delay-in-sandf-review-costing-armed-forces-minister/.

13 Jakkie Cilliers, 'The 2014 South African Defence Review: Rebuilding after Years of Abuse, Neglect and Decay', Institute for Security Studies, June 2014, pp. 4–5.

14 International Institute for Strategic Studies, Military Balance+, November 2017.

15 Alex Vines, 'South Africa's Politics of Peace and Security in Africa', *South African Journal of International Affairs*, vol. 17, no. 1, 2010, p. 61.

16 *Ibid.*

17 Chris Alden and Maxi Schoeman, 'South Africa in the Company of Giants: The Search for Leadership in a Transforming Global Order', *International Affairs*, vol. 89, no. 1, 2013, p. 122.

18 Hussein Solomon, 'South Africa in Africa: A case of high expectations for peace', *South African Journal of International Affairs*, vol. 17, no. 2, 2010, p. 144.

19 *Ibid.*, p. 142.

20 Alden and Schoeman, 'In the Company of Giants', p. 122

21 Lucy Dunderdale, 'South Africa's Peacekeeping Activities in Africa', Southern African Catholic Bishop's Conference, 2013, p. 4.

22 'Sixty-two Per Cent of SANDF Facilities in Unacceptable Condition',

defenceWeb, 7 March 2014, http://www.defenceweb.co.za/index.php?option=com_content&view=article&id=33889:sixty-two-percent-of-sandf-facilities-in-unacceptable-condition&catid=111:sa-defence&Itemid=242.

23 Wendell Roelf, 'South African Military in Critical Decline, Review Says', Reuters, 25 March 2014, http://www.reuters.com/article/us-safrica-defence-exclusive-idUSBREA2O10U20140325.

24 Cited in Heleta, 'Securitising Humanitarian Assistance and Post-conflict Reconstruction in Africa', p. 8.

25 Tshaba Tjemolane, Theo Needling and Albert Schoeman, 'South Africa's Foreign Policy and Africa: Continental Partner or Hegemon?', *Africa Review*, vol. 4, no. 2, 2012, pp. 95–6.

26 South African Department of Defence, *South African Defence Review 2014* (Pretoria: South African Department of Defence, 2014), p. 9.5.

27 Cilliers, 'The 2014 South African Defence Review', p. 5.

28 South African Department of Defence, *South African Defence Review 2014*, p. 9.9.

29 *Ibid.*

30 Brown, 'Once a Major Continental Force, South Africa's Military at a Crossroads'.

31 Centre for Conflict Resolution, *Post-Apartheid South Africa's Foreign Policy after Two Decades*, p. 22.

32 South African Department of Defence, *South African Defence Review 2014* (Pretoria: South African Department of Defence, 2014), p. 3.10.

33 *Ibid.*, p. 1X.

34 *Ibid.*, p. 9.2.

35 Samir Puri, *Fighting and Negotiating with Armed Groups: The Difficulty of Securing Strategic Outcomes* (Abingdon:

Routledge for the IISS, 2016).

36 *Ibid.*, pp. 3–4.

37 *Ibid.*, p. 4.

38 Helmoed Romer Heitman, 'Challenges Ahead if SA Wants to Be Africa's Military Superpower', *ISS Today*, 4 August 2014, , https://issafrica.org/iss-today/challenges-ahead-if-sa-wants-to-be-africas-military-superpower.

39 *Ibid.*

40 Mills, 'An Option of Difficulties?', p. 24.

41 *South African Defence Review 2014*, 'Chairperson's Overview', p. 1X.

42 Cilliers, 'The 2014 South African Defence Review', p. 7.

43 Wyndham Hartley, 'Minister Sets Five-year Target to Fix Defence', *Business Day*, 24 July 2014, http://www.bdlive.co.za/national/2014/07/24/minister-sets-five-year-target-to-fix-defence.

44 Wyndham Hartley, 'Report on Critical State of SANDF Gathers Dust', *Business Day*, 30 September 2014, http://www.bdlive.co.za/national/2014/09/30/report-on-critical-state-of-sandf-gathers-dust.

45 Abel Esterhuyse, 'Money Has Little to Do with Why South Africa's Military Is Failing to Do Its Job', *Conversation*, 19 July 2017, https://theconversation.com/money-has-little-to-do-with-why-south-africas-military-is-failing-to-do-its-job-81216.

46 Heleta, 'Securitising Humanitarian Assistance and Post-conflict Reconstruction in Africa', p. 14.

47 Prisloo, 'The Security Dilemma Evident in South Africa's Policy Towards Africa', p. 87.

48 Mills, 'An Option of Difficulties?', p. 23.

49 Peter Fabricius, 'Are We Seeing the Emergence of a New "Zuma Doctrine" on Africa?', Institute of Security Studies, 2 May 2013, https://issafrica.org/crimehub/iss-today/are-we-

seeing-the-emergence-of-a-new-zuma-doctrine-on-africa.

50 Heleta, 'Securitising Humanitarian Assistance and Post-conflict Reconstruction in Africa', p. 7.

51 Hartley, 'Minister Sets Five-year Target to Fix Defence'.

52 Hartley, 'Newly Formed Defence Committee Urged to Consider Review'.

53 Fabricius, 'Are We Seeing the Emergence of a New "Zuma Doctrine" on Africa?'.

54 'South Africa Pulls Out of Unamid in Darfur', *Dabanga*, 25 February 2016, https://www.dabangasudan.org/en/all-news/article/south-africa-pulls-out-of-unamid-in-darfur-un-official.

55 Brown, 'Once a Major Continental Force, South Africa's Military at a Crossroads'.

56 *Ibid.*

57 *Ibid.*

58 Pelani Phakgadi, 'SANDF: We Don't Have the Budget to Keep SA Safe', Eyewitness News, 17 July 2017, http://ewn.co.za/2017/07/17/sandf-we-don-t-the-budget-to-keep-sa-safe.

59 John Stupart, 'Diverted Funds Puts Soldiers at Risk', *Mail & Guardian*, 30 June 2017, https://mg.co.za/article/2017-06-30-00-diverted-funds-puts-soldiers-at-risk.

60 Adam Quinn, 'The Art of Declining Politely: Obama's Prudent Presidency and the Waning of American Power', *International Affairs*, vol. 87, no. 4, 2011, p. 803.

61 Jakkie Cilliers, Julia Schünemann and Jonathan D. Moyer, 'Power and Influence in Africa: Algeria, Egypt, Ethiopia, Nigeria and South Africa', Institute of Security Studies, March 2015, p. 18.

62 Brown, 'Once a Major Continental Force, South Africa's Military at a Crossroads'.

63 Peter Fabricius, 'SA Should First Sort Out Its Own Backyard', *ISS Today*, 20 July 2017, https://issafrica.org/iss-today/sa-should-first-sort-out-its-own-backyard.

64 Guy Martin, 'Defence Budget Shrinks', defenceWeb, 6 March 2017, http://www.defenceweb.co.za/index.php?option=com_content&view=article&id=47022.

Conclusion

1 Joseph S. Nye, *Is the American Century Over?* (Cambridge: Polity Press, 2015).

2 J.E. Spence, 'South Africa: an African exception or just another country?', *Conflict, Security & Development*, vol. 7, no. 2, 2007, pp. 341-347.

3 Olusola Ogunnubi and Ufo Okeke-Uzodike, 'Can Nigeria Be Africa's Hegemon?', *African Security Review*, vol. 25, no. 2, 2016, p. 110.

4 Jakkie Cilliers, Julia Schünemann and Jonathan D. Moyer, 'Power and Influence in Africa: Algeria, Egypt, Ethiopia, Nigeria and South Africa', Institute of Security Studies, March 2015, p. 22.

5 Harry Verhoeven et al. cited in Savo Heleta, 'Securitising humanitarian assistance and post-conflict reconstruction in Africa: A critical review of South Africa's new defence policy', *African Security Review*, vol. 25,

no. 1, 2016, p. 14.

6 Anthoni van Nieuwkerk, 'A Review of South Africa's Peace Diplomacy Since 1994', in Chris Landsberg and Jo-Ansie van Wyk (eds), *South African Foreign Policy Review: Volume 1* (Cape Town: Africa Institute of South Africa, 2012), p. 101.

7 *South African Defence Review 2014*, Chapter 7, 'Regional and Continental Peace and Security', p. 75.

8 Chris Landsberg, 'South Africa and the Making of the African Union and NEPAD: Mbeki's "Progressive African Agenda"', in Adekeye Adebajo, Adebayo Adedeji and Chris Landsberg (eds), *South Africa in Africa: The Post-Apartheid Era* (Scottsville: University of KwaZulu-Natal Press, 2007), p. 212.

9 Randall Schweller cited in Maxi Schoeman, 'South Africa as an Emerging Power: From Label to Status Consistency', *South African Journal of International Affairs*, vol. 22, no. 4, p. 441, footnote 2.

10 Tony Leon, 'Where in the World is South Africa?', *South African Journal of International Affairs*, vol. 20, no. 3, 2013, p. 447.

11 'African powerhouses Kenya and South Africa can tag team and win the wealth game', *Mail & Guardian*, 11 September 2015, http://mgafrica.com/article/2015-09-09-african-powerhouses-can-create-wealth-together.

12 James Hamill, 'Kagame's Rwanda Presents South Africa with Delicate Balancing Act', *World Politics Review*, 24 March 2014, http://www.worldpoliticsreview.com/articles/13648/kagame-s-rwanda-presents-south-africa-with-delicate-balancing-act.

13 Chris Landsberg, 'Nigeria–South Africa Tensions Leave African

Leadership Gap', *World Politics Review*, 18 April 2012, p. 2, http://www.worldpoliticsreview.com/articles/11857/nigeria-south-africa-tensions-leave-african-leadership-gap.

14 Alfredo Tjiurimo Hengari, 'Pitfalls and Prospects: Nigeria and South Africa in Africa', *South African Institute of International Affairs*, 23 March 2015, http://www.saiia.org.za/opinion-analysis/pitfalls-and-prospects-nigeria-and-south-africa-in-africa.

15 Maxi Schoeman, 'South Africa as an Emerging Power: From Label to Status Consistency', p. 434.

16 James Hamill, 'Limited Detente: The Challenges to Repairing South Africa–Nigeria Ties', *World Politics Review*, 17 March 2016, p. 4, http://www.worldpoliticsreview.com/articles/18236/limited-detente-the-challenges-to-repairing-south-africa-nigeria-ties.

17 Peter Fabricius, 'Back to the Future for ANC Foreign Policy?', Institute of Security Studies, June 2015.

18 Graham Evans, 'The End of the Rainbow', *World Today*, vol. 55, no. 1, January 1999, p. 10.

19 Jakkie Cilliers, 'Life Beyond BRICS? South Africa's Future Foreign Policy Interests', Institute for Security Studies and Frederick S. Pardee Center for International Studies, June 2017, p. 14.

20 Nic Cheeseman, 'Will Mnangagwa usher in a new democracy? The view from Zimbabwe', *The Conversation*, 23 November 2017, https://theconversation.com/will-mnangagwa-usher-in-a-new-democracy-the-view-from-zimbabwe-88023.

21 Evans, 'The End of the Rainbow', p. 10.

22 Stephen Grootes, 'Things fall apart: Downward pressure as ANC

government loses its grip', *Daily Maverick*, 25 October 2016, http://www.dailymaverick.co.za/article/2016-10-24-things-fall-apart-downward-pressure-as-anc-government-loses-its-grip/#.WBJaZfkrLIU.

23 James Hamill, 'A New Leader for South Africa's ANC Won't Guarantee a Break from Zuma', *World Politics Review*, 5 July 2017, http://www.worldpoliticsreview.com/articles/22616/a-new-leader-for-south-africa-s-anc-won-t-guarantee-a-break-from-zuma.

24 'We refuse to be silent on contaminated ANC – Ramaphosa', *Politicsweb*, 8 May 2017, http://politicsweb.co.za/news-and-analysis/we-refuse-to-be-silent-on-contaminated-anc--ramaph; and Dineo Bendile, 'Leaders' Behaviour behind ANC's Decay', *Mail & Guardian*, 30 June 2017, https://mg.co.za/article/2017-06-30-00-leaders-behaviour-behind-ancs-decay/.

25 Susan Booysen, 'Why the ANC may be stumbling closer to its most serious split yet', *The Conversation*, 29 June 2017, https://theconversation.com/why-the-anc-may-be-stumbling-closer-to-its-most-serious-split-yet-80282.

INDEX

A

Abacha, Sani 23, 26
Abegunrin, Olayiwola 30, 81, 82, 88
Adams, Simon 37
Addis Ababa (Ethiopia) 98
Adebajo, Adekeye 21, 25
African Capacity for Immediate Response to Crises 112, 124
African National Congress (S Africa) 20, 29, 30, 34, 36, 37, 39, 54, 55, 66, 68, 71, 73, 78, 80, 81, 87, 88, 90, 91, 92, 96, 104, 105, 121, 122, 123, 124, 130, 131, 137, 139, 140, 141
African Peace and Security Architecture 26
African Peer Review Mechanism 26, 42
African Renaissance 26, 27, 28, 30, 31, 33, 53, 79, 80, 91, 97, 101, 128, 131
African Solidarity Conference 98
African Union 19, 26, 30, 37, 42, 48, 51, 52, 73, 75, 77, 98, 108, 112, 136
  African Standby Force 108, 112
  AU Commission 51, 52, 136
Ahwireng-Obeng, Fred 58
Alden, Chris 43, 49, 88, 104
Algeria 25, 114, 134, 135
al-Shabaab (Somalia) 111
Angola 18, 23, 24, 42, 56, 57, 62, 70, 71, 72, 94, 99, 111, 114, 127, 134, 135, 138
apartheid 10, 11, 14, 52, 54, 55, 56, 60, 69, 79, 81, 86, 87, 105, 107, 112
Argentina 85
Arusha Accords 19

B

Bangui (CAR) 117
al-Bashir, Omar 31, 37, 38, 39, 72, 129, 133
BASIC group 47
Belarus 30
Benin 129

Bentley, Kristina 69
Boko Haram (Nigeria) 62, 94, 95, 111
Bolivia 129
Bond, Patrick 29
Botha, P.W. 10
Botswana 13, 57, 58, 99, 100, 103
Bozizé, François 117
Brazil 35, 36, 40, 47, 63, 64, 83, 93, 103, 129
BRICS group 35, 36, 37, 40, 41, 47, 49, 50, 65, 80, 93, 128, 129, 132, 133, 138
  Leaders–Africa Dialogue Forum 50
  New Development Bank 50
    African Regional Centre 50
Buhari, Muhammadu 94, 137
Burundi 19, 72, 77, 98, 108, 115

C

Canada 29
Central African Republic 20, 74, 109, 117, 118, 123, 125
Chile 85
China 33, 35, 36, 47, 63, 64, 93, 129, 137
Cilliers, Jakkie 43, 57, 89, 95, 112, 121
Clinton, Bill 25
Cold War 29, 60, 111, 132, 137
Common Market for Eastern and Southern Africa 60
Commonwealth 23
Constellation of Southern African States 10
COP-21 47
Côte d'Ivoire 19, 20, 72, 73, 74, 118, 136
Crocker, Chester 81
Cuba 25, 103

D

Darfur (Sudan) 128
Democratic Alliance (S Africa) 123
Democratic Republic of the Congo 18, 19, 23, 24, 42, 65, 72, 73, 74, 76, 77, 98, 99, 103, 108,

111, 114, 115, 118, 124, 126, 127, 138
St Sylvestre deal 72
Development Bank of Southern Africa 63
Dlamini-Zuma, Nkosazana 36, 47, 51
Dube, Memory 89
Dunderdale, Lucy 115, 116
Durban (S Africa) 50, 53

E
East African Community 60
Economic Community of Central African
  States 74
Economic Community of West African States
  74
Economic Freedom Fighters (S Africa)
  123
Economist 18, 37, 110
Egypt 85, 134, 135
Eritrea 19, 108, 111, 135
Eskom (S Africa) 63
Ethiopia 19, 51, 77, 94, 108, 111, 134, 135
European Union 48, 56, 59
Evans, Graham 22, 105, 138

F
Fabricius, Peter 123
Fitch (US) 85
France 29, 37, 75, 118

G
G8 29, 47
G20 41, 47, 48, 49
Gabon 51
Gadhafi, Muammar 27, 28, 36, 37, 71, 72, 128
Gbagbo, Laurent 19, 72
Germany 103
Gerson, Michael 30
Gevisser, Mark 69
Ghana 25, 94, 134, 135
Gilmour, Christopher 61
Global Railway Engineering Consortium (S
  Africa) 31
Global South 28, 33, 40, 41, 80, 104, 128, 129,
  140
Gordhan, Pravin 84, 85
Gordon, Steven 53
Guinea 103
Guinea-Bissau 103
Gulube, Sam 125

H
Habib, Adam 10, 28
Hainan Island (China) 40
Heitman, Helmoed-Römer 120, 121, 124, 126
Heleta, Savo 96, 97
Hendricks, Cheryl 98

I
Ibrahim, Ibrahim 90
India 35, 36, 40, 47, 64, 93, 103, 129

India–Brazil–South Africa forum 40, 41, 47,
  103
International Criminal Court 24, 31, 37, 38, 39,
  129, 133, 135
International Futures Base Case 93
International Monetary Fund 27, 48, 84, 95
  Executive Board for sub-Saharan Africa 48
Iran 25, 30
Iraq 27

J
Japan 88, 103
Johannesburg (S Africa) 37, 50, 53, 87, 95
Jonathan, Goodluck 62, 136

K
Kabila, Joseph 72
Kabila, Laurent 23, 24, 111
Kagame, Paul 136
Kagwanja, Peter 13
Kasai (DRC) 72
Kayuni, Happy 92
Kenya 51, 58, 60, 62, 73, 94, 134, 135, 136
Keohane, Robert 12
Khampepe Report 32
Kimberley Process 77
Klerk, F.W. de 11, 55
Kraxberger, Brennan 17

L
Landsberg, Chris 137
Lemarchand, René 74
Leon, Tony 135
Lesotho 13, 18, 24, 58, 74, 77, 98, 99, 100, 101,
  127
Libya 20, 25, 27, 28, 36, 37, 70, 71, 72, 118, 128,
  136
  government of national unity 71, 72, 73, 75
Lockerbie bombing 1988 28, 128
Lord's Resistance Army (Uganda) 111
Lucey, Amanda 98

M
M-23 (DRC) 118
McClaughry, Paul 17
McGowan, Patrick 58
Mali 118
Mandela, Nelson 17, 18, 20, 21, 22, 23, 24, 25,
  28, 29, 30, 42, 68, 79, 81, 90, 94, 107, 108, 127
Mantashe, Gwede 141
Mapisa-Nqakula, Nosiviwe 121
Maputo Development Corridor 76
Martin, Guy 126
Masters, Lesley 102, 104
Mbeki, Thabo 14, 18, 19, 24, 25, 26, 27, 28, 29,
  30, 31, 32, 33, 34, 35, 36, 40, 48, 66, 71, 89,
  101, 104, 108, 127, 128, 131, 136, 140
van der Merwe, Sue 63
Mexico 47, 85
Meyer, Roelf 119, 120

Mills, Greg 20, 123
Mobutu, Sese Seko 23
Moody's (US) 85
Movement for Democratic Change
    (Zimbabwe) 31, 32, 71
Moyer, Jonathan 43, 89, 95
Mozambique 19, 25, 57, 76, 77, 99, 103
Mozambique Channel 124
MTN (S Africa) 62
Mugabe, Robert 27, 32, 35, 36, 71, 72, 138, 139

N

Namibia 13, 24, 42, 57, 58, 99, 100, 103, 111
Nathan, Laurie 33
National Union for the Total Independence of
    Angola 23, 71
NATO 36, 118
Needling, Theo 62
Nel, Phillip 59
Nelson Mandela Bay (S Africa) 87
Netherlands 28
New Diplomacy 11, 55
New Partnership for Africa's Development 26,
    27, 33, 42, 67, 101, 128
van Nieuwkerk, Anthoni 134
Nigeria 18, 23, 24, 25, 42, 44, 45, 50, 51, 52, 57,
    62, 74, 93, 94, 95, 96, 98, 127, 133, 134, 135,
    136, 137
Nkoana-Mashabane, Maite 39, 48, 63, 124
Nkurunziza, Pierre 72
North Korea 30, 139
Nuclear Non-Proliferation Treaty 24, 127

O

Obasanjo, Olusegun 136
Ogunnubi, Olusola 43
Olivier, Gerrit 27
Organisation of African Unity 23, 26, 51

P

Pahad, Aziz 107
People's Movement for the Liberation of
    Angola 71
le Pere, Garth 49, 53, 82, 88, 101
PetroSA (Sudan) 31
Ping, Jean 51
Popular Movement for the Liberation of
    Angola 23
post-conflict reconstruction and development
    96, 97, 98, 99
Presidential Infrastructure Championing
    Initiative 76
Pretoria (S Africa) 87
Pretoria Agreement 19
Putin, Vladimir 35

Q

Qobo, Mzukisi 89, 137
Quinn, Adam 125

R

Ramaphosa, Cyril 141
Rautenbach, George 64
Reagan, Ronald 81
Rome Statute 24, 38
Roux, Andre 124
Russia 35, 36, 93, 129
Rwanda 23, 51, 103, 111, 136

S

Saro-Wiwa, Ken 23
Schoeman, Albert 43, 45, 62
Schoeman, Maxi 92, 104
Schünemann, Julia 43, 89, 95
Schweller, Randall 135
Scotland (UK) 28
Shillinger, Kurt 70
Shoprite (S Africa) 60
Sierra Leone 103
Sisulu, Lindiwe 108, 114
Smith, Karen 78, 109
Solomon, Hussein 114
South Africa
    African Renaissance Fund 97, 101
    Building a Better World 40
    Defence Review 2014 44, 109, 111, 112, 115,
        131, 134
    Defence Review Committee 119
    Department of International Relations and
        Cooperation 34, 40, 58, 74, 86, 90, 102, 104
    Department of Trade and Industry 58, 63,
        102
    destabilisation 11
    Development Bank of Southern Africa 96
    Diplomatic Immunities and Privileges Act
        38
    foreign direct investment 64
    Global Political Agreement 71
    Growth, Employment and Redistribution
        strategy 29
    High Court 38
    Human Rights Commission 54
    Human Sciences Research Council 96
    Independent Electoral Commission 96
    Industrial Development Corporation 63, 96
    National Development Plan 49, 57, 82, 89,
        102, 123
    New Diplomacy 11, 55
    Public Protector 66
    South African National Defence Force 14,
        15, 44, 107, 108, 109, 110, 111, 112, 114, 115,
        116, 117, 118, 119, 120, 121, 122, 123, 124,
        125, 126, 131
    Statistics South Africa 83
    Stock Exchange 95
    Transformation 81
South African Development Partnership
    Agency 97, 101, 102, 103
    Partnership Development Fund 102
Southall, Roger 69

Southern African Customs Union 13, 58, 60, 75, 93, 96, 99, 100, 102, 131
Southern African Development Community 13, 19, 24, 25, 31, 42, 48, 56, 57, 58, 59, 60, 68, 74, 77, 79, 93, 99, 108, 109, 114, 126, 129, 139
  SADC Brigade 108, 114
South Sudan 20, 96, 98, 103
Spence, J.E. 20, 54, 132
Spoornet (S Africa) 64
Sri Lanka 129
Standard & Poor's (US) 85
Sudan 31, 37, 72, 108, 128, 129, 133, 135
  Darfur 19, 31, 38
Sudanese Railway Corporation 31
Sudan People's Liberation Movement 20
Swaziland 13, 19, 42, 43, 58, 74, 99, 100, 101, 138
Sweden 103
Syria 129, 139

T
Tambulasi, Richard 92
Tanzania 25, 62, 134, 135
Taylor, Ian 26, 59, 63, 67
Tjemolane, Tshaba 62
Tjiurimo, Alfredo 52
Transparency International 94

U
Uganda 23, 51, 111, 135
United Kingdom 29, 75, 128
United Nations 19, 27, 29, 30, 36, 39, 41, 47, 52, 72, 73, 77, 94, 99, 110, 114, 118, 120, 125, 132, 133, 136
  Ad Hoc Working Group on Conflict Prevention and Resolution in Africa 47
  Force Intervention Brigade 118
  Human Development Index 94, 110
  Human Rights Council 30, 39, 72
  Organization Stabilization Mission in the DRC 19, 114, 118
  Responsibility to Protect 29, 30
  Security Council 27, 30, 36, 39, 41, 47, 52, 77, 132, 136
    Resolution 1973 36, 37
United States 25, 27, 28, 29, 37, 45, 51, 64, 78, 81, 83, 103, 128, 132, 137
  African Crisis Response Initiative 25
Uzbekistan 30

V
Vickers, Brendan 63, 64, 65, 90
Vietnam 103, 129
Vines, Alex 114
Vorster, B.J. 10

W
Windhoek Treaty 31
World Bank 28

World Economic Forum 84
World Summit 29, 30
World Trade Organisation 28, 41, 48, 60
  Doha Round 60

Y
Yanacopulos, Helen 102

Z
Zaire (See Democratic Republic of the Congo) 18, 23, 127
Zambia 138
Zimbabwe 19, 24, 27, 28, 30, 31, 32, 33, 35, 36, 42, 43, 71, 72, 73, 74, 77, 111, 128, 135, 138, 139
Zimbabwean African National Union–Patriotic Front 28, 31, 32, 35, 71, 74
Zuma, Jacob 9, 14, 17, 19, 33, 34, 35, 36, 37, 38, 40, 43, 48, 49, 54, 62, 66, 67, 68, 72, 84, 87, 90, 92, 95, 97, 98, 101, 102, 120, 121, 122, 123, 124, 127, 128, 136, 137, 140

Adelphi books are published eight times a year by Routledge Journals, an imprint of Taylor & Francis, 4 Park Square, Milton Park, Abingdon, Oxfordshire OX14 4RN, UK.

A subscription to the institution print edition, ISSN 1944-5571, includes free access for any number of concurrent users across a local area network to the online edition, ISSN 1944-558X. Taylor & Francis has a flexible approach to subscriptions enabling us to match individual libraries' requirements. This journal is available via a traditional institutional subscription (either print with free online access, or online-only at a discount) or as part of our libraries, subject collections or archives. For more information on our sales packages please visit www.tandfonline.com/page/librarians.

2018 Annual Adelphi Subscription Rates			
Institution	£719	US$1,262	€1,063
Individual	£254	US$434	€347
Online only	£629	US$1,104	€930

Dollar rates apply to subscribers outside Europe. Euro rates apply to all subscribers in Europe except the UK and the Republic of Ireland where the pound sterling price applies. All subscriptions are payable in advance and all rates include postage. Journals are sent by air to the USA, Canada, Mexico, India, Japan and Australasia. Subscriptions are entered on an annual basis, i.e. January to December. Payment may be made by sterling cheque, dollar cheque, international money order, National Giro, or credit card (Amex, Visa, Mastercard).

For a complete and up-to-date guide to Taylor & Francis journals and books publishing programmes, and details of advertising in our journals, visit our website: http://www.tandfonline.com.

Ordering information:
USA/Canada: Taylor & Francis Inc., Journals Department, 530 Walnut Street, Suite 850, Philadelphia, PA 19106, USA. **UK/Europe/Rest of World:** Routledge Journals, T&F Customer Services, T&F Informa UK Ltd., Sheepen Place, Colchester, Essex, CO3 3LP, UK.

Advertising enquiries to:
USA/Canada: The Advertising Manager, Taylor & Francis Inc., 530 Walnut Street, Suite 850, Philadelphia, PA 19106, USA. Tel: +1 (800) 354 1420. Fax: +1 (215) 207 0050. **UK/Europe/Rest of World**: The Advertising Manager, Routledge Journals, Taylor & Francis, 4 Park Square, Milton Park, Abingdon, Oxfordshire OX14 4RN, UK. Tel: +44 (0) 20 7017 6000. Fax: +44 (0) 20 7017 6336.